Notorious

Notorious

Poetic Travels
of the Fierce
Feminine

LIZANNE CORBIT

Notorious: Poetic Travels of the Fierce Feminine
Published by Temenos Publishing
Denver, CO

Names: Corbit M.A., Lizanne. author.
Title: Notorious : poetic travels of the fierce feminine /
Lizanne Corbit.
Description: Denver [Colorado] : Temenos Publishing, 2019. Paper-
back. Also being published as an ebook.
Identifiers: ISBN: 978-0-692-04004-1
Subjects: LCSH: Poetry. | Metaphysics.
BISAC: LITERATURE & FICTION / Poetry / Women Authors |
RELIGION & SPIRITUALITY / New Age & Spirituality /
Goddesses
Classification: LCC PS306 | DDC 811.6–dc22

Cover and Interior design by Andrea Costantine
Cover Artwork by Hülya Özdemir Coka

QUANTITY PURCHASES: Schools, companies, professional
groups, clubs, and other organizations may qualify for special
terms when ordering quantities of this title. For information, email
info@temenospublishing.com.

TEMENOS
PUBLISHING

I dedicate this book to the "Fierce Feminine"
and to all the courageous women and men
who stand in their power,
who choose to live from their brilliance,
who bless others in their suffering,
who break the spell of silence,
and who roar with a mighty call for truth and love
to prevail in these transformational times.

Contents

Prologue

The heroine's journey is as old as time and as deeply embedded in the marrow of our bones and instinctual wisdom as the DNA of our being. We each have gloriousness that deserves to be claimed and celebrated.

In these changing and challenging times, we have been called out of our wounds, our powerlessness, and our silence. Our divine origins have been calling us with a sacred roar to stand up, stand in, and stand for our beauty, worth, value, and our goodness, and to be recognized and honored as the sacred, sassy, sweet beings that we each are.

It is our basic human right to be seen, valued, and treated fairly, kindly, and lovingly. We all deserve kindness, compassion, and love. It makes no difference where we come from, what gender, what color, or what persuasion we are. We all deserve to be treated with basic human decency, respect, and compassion.

This poetry is the result of my initiation by the Fierce Feminine. Each stage along the journey was essential, from listening to and embracing the call, to seeking and wandering in landscapes that were both terrifying and terrorizing, to lifting the veil of survival and digging deep for the hidden gems of my essence and reclaiming the unique brilliance of my being, to becoming a card-carrying revolutionary for the sacred cause of love. Each and every step on this journey has had its challenges and its gifts. I have faltered and failed, and I have triumphed and sung praises for the blessings along the way.

Throughout this journey, I have had to call upon my deepest strength and my fiercest love to challenge the demons that threatened to keep me prisoner and throw away the key, condemning me to an age-old lifetime of shame and fear. Fear, oh fear—that illusive, soul-freezing voice that made my skin crawl and forced me to shrink into the dark corner and get as small as possible, so as to not be found out and exposed.

The tempering, testing, and trials of owning my brilliance has been as amazing as it has been devastating. To own myself in all my notoriousness, all the old beliefs, untruths, and strategies of silence had to be devastated in order to remove the eons of crusted-over dirt and expose the gems of my essence.

Each of us has our own brilliance that has been hidden away in the dark, waiting to be mined and released from the wounds of our forbearers and brought into the light of day to sparkle and shine as the beautiful gems that we are. Being a wounded feminine is nothing new. We've all been dismissed, demeaned, judged, violated, raped, and silenced. For millennium, we have experienced power over us and been made to feel shame for being a woman. We have survived centuries of abuse of our hearts, our bodies, and of our souls. Our brilliance may have gone underground at times in order to survive, but it has always, yes always, been there every step of the way. Forever and always, just waiting for us to hear the sacred roar to come home to our strength, our power, and our divine beauty and grace.

Although the journey ahead is not for the faint of heart, I promise you it will be well worth it. Traveling this path of love will awaken and activate the Fierce Feminine in you. She is the powerful warrior of love that all of us need and that our world invites us to embrace to bring our brilliant, beautiful essence back from the buried depths into the full light of day.

The Fierce Feminine will always be our guide and warrior of the heart, fighting her way through the dogma of being demeaned and dismissed. She will forever rain down blessings upon blessings of love.

Yet, once the Fierce Feminine is activated, our work is far from over. We have, we can, and we will continue to travel this transformational journey. We need not be afraid or shrink away from this calling. The guiding light in every moment of trepidation and darkness is love—always love. We are love; we give love; we share love; we desire, deserve, and demand love. Love is the elixir and the balm for healing the ills of the world. Amen for love. Amen to love.

Rock On Fierce Feminine Love Warriors

Welcome to the Revolution of Love!

Note from the Author

As a psychotherapist over the last thirty years, I have been deeply and irrevocably changed by the courage I bear witness to on a daily basis. I am always, yes always, gob smacked in amazement at what the power of love does to heal even the nastiest of wounds.

I have had the privilege and honor to be a part of some kickass, courageous, transformational work by both men and women. These courageous seekers have answered the call, traveled the journey, lifted the veil of survival, dug deep, sifted, cleared away the debris, been tempered, tested, and tried, and fought the inner demons and outer dogma to reclaim their beautiful essences.

It's been the power of love that has done the healing. It is women with their arms embracing, hands held high, mirroring beauty, nurturing vulnerability, and honoring and celebrating each other's beauty that has been the transformational elixir. It takes the fiercest of the feminine to create a sacred and safe container in which to do this transformative work. And work it is—hard work, soft work, loving work, truth work, compelling work, confounding work, but always and forever transformative work.

Becoming your notorious self isn't for the faint of heart. It is for the heart warriors with their loving hearts that hold, heal, and honor, so that we each may return our birthright to its rightful place. Coming home to our unique, special, beyond-measure beauty and essence is our birthright.

This journey tears the untruths away one veil at a time and lands us smack dab in the treasures of our essence. We all in our heart of hearts want to be seen and revel and delight in our own unique brand of brilliance. We were born for this.

So, welcome aboard this heart-quaking, soul-shaking, spirit-reveling journey. Oftentimes, it is frightening and arduous, but we can just as easily be awestruck and bow down in reverence to our deepest truth and beauty as it is revealed to us along our way.

One

Embracing the Call

Wading through the wasteland,
listening for the deep abiding truth
in the cacophony of chaos

Bejeweled Morning

Sweet surrender to the bird song of the Beloved
Singing ever so softly the morning rising
Beloved one surrounding me with the serenade of
the Universe's delight
Exchanging awe and oohs as twilight awakens
the world

Alabaster sky peaking up over the darkness
Revealing one beautiful shoulder at a time
Seducing us with her beauty

Raven calling for us to awaken
Their caws always campaigning for God's delight
The night has left us once again and we are alone
The light of day revealing to us our instructions

Bejeweled ruby-red sky, dropping promises for
the day
Like gems from the sky being tossed here and
there
With us scrambling for "just the one"
Which will guarantee our riches for the coming
adventure

Uncommon quietness before the dawn of our new
day

Ensuring surrender to the wonders of the world
  before it fully awakens
Promising beauty at every turn, around every
  corner
With each blink of an eye
In every heartbeat and step taken

Open your heart to the wonders of the world
For they are the treasures for all to partake of
Dip your hand in and pluck out your jewel
And let your heart be filled with wonder

Let yourself be reminded of your wonder
As the light of day shines on you and sparkles
With the sweetest bejeweled wonder of you today

The Winds of Change

The winds of change caress you sweetly
  in the morning's refreshing breeze called love
The winds of change rustle your thoughts
    like leaves in a tree, letting you know they are
    there
The winds of change rattle the windows of your
    soul
    shaking them open, reminding you that your
    vulnerability needs tending to

The winds of change sweep the streets of debris
  and scatter the untruths hither and thither
The winds of change shake the foundation of
    your being
    as gale-force winds blow and wail while you
    hunker down safely inside
The winds of change whip and twirl fiercely
    rotating and uprooting all that you have known

The winds of change settle and soften
    sweetly caressing your cheek in the middle of
    the night's sleep
    reminding you that you are always in love's
    gentle embrace

The winds of change catch you as you fall from
    the sky
    holding you like a feather ever so gently floating
    you to the ground
    of your truest being

The winds of change whip up and blast you with
    a breathtaking reminder
    that it is forever guiding you home
    and stirring the pot of change

For new life to be born in your heart
    you must partake in the breath of the Beloved
Wind whipping
Heart stirring
Soul singing
Spirit reveling
Breath of God

You may now wish for a tornado to carry you to
    Kansas
All you ever have to do is click your ruby red
    slippers
    and say home is where I belong and
You will be magically transported by the Breath of
    God

Discern

Discern the wild from the wicked
Discern the invitation from the call to do
Discern the heartfelt from the seduction of success
Discern the pull of the peaceful within from the
    push of the chaotic outside
Discern the essential wild one from the
    established craft maker
Discern the solitude of silence from the invitation
    to speak without thought
Discern the quiet beauty from the glimmer of
    falsehood
Discern the wizened human from the trying-too-
    hard court jester
Discern the soulful acknowledgment from the
    alleluia of praise
Discern the deep rich feminine from the power-
    packed masculine
Discern the everlasting presence from the flash-in-
    the-pan of insight
Discern the holy ground from the elevated false
    altars
Discern the hallowed of the everyday from the
    charisma of the moment

Discern, Oh Notorious Wild One
For the truth lies in the light underneath the
    bushel basket
Waiting and ready to be set free

Life Is a Prayer

Life is a prayer

Sometimes it's a fervent prayer for something
   deep inside to be met
Sometimes it's a petition for The Divine's will to
   be done and a path made clear
Sometimes it's a heartfelt, tear-filled whisper for
   love to return swiftly
   so you can land softly
Sometimes it's a full-on rant and raving demand
   for understanding
   in the chaotic shambles and shockwaves of
   change

Sometimes it's a soft whisper of gratitude
   deeply felt as a wish is finally granted
Sometimes it's a focused intention with laser-like
   intensity for a specific request
Sometimes it's a chanting repetition to soothe the
   weary-hearted soul
Sometimes it's a full-blown revival, clapping and
   praising, "Can I get a Hallelujah!"
Sometimes life is an acknowledgment of beauty in
   this very moment
   with a simple, and yet, oh so powerful "Amen"

At all times life is a prayer in the making
All we have to do is go within
   and acknowledge with reverence
   our birthright as *inspiritus* beings

We are the prayer in motion
   a divine comedy or drama
   whichever is your choice
But we are divinity in creation
   a prayer for the ages in who we are and
   how we live
I bow in reverence to your deep, rich life as a
   prayer in the making

Some of my favorite prayers are:
Deep Peace
Oh my God!
Holy Crap!
Wow!
Amen
Hallelujah!
Yippee Ki-yo Ki-yay
Fuck!
Thank you

I didn't say prayer is always pretty
Sometimes it's all we can do to utter one word
Just one word

In that one word we call on the Universe
and it conspires to support us in whatever we
need in that exact moment

Soror Mystica

Soror Mystica
Soul Sisters

Soul Shaking
Mask Making

We make masks
We leave the old for the becoming
We cast the mold for being
We fill the soul being behind the old undoing
We free the essence from the nothingness
We open to the becoming of who we are
We welcome the blessings of our gifts revealing
We delight in the form and shape the Mother
    mirrors to us
We dance with the ancestors and sing ourselves
    alive
We bow in reverence to her Majesty's presence
We receive the gift she bestows upon us
We pray for the guidance along our travels
We commit to honor ourselves as we would
    honor the Mother
We choose to be her emissaries of love
Showering light on ourselves and being bathed in
    her spirit

Enlightening and enlivening our very soul
We will be all that we are here to be
Amen

Power Mongers

Dear One
Hear my cries in the middle of the night
Hear my love song for peace on earth
Hear my wail of grief at the injustice as the people
   of my heart are killed mercilessly
Hear my scream of shock as I collapse in despair
   at the killing of innocents
   with one pull of a trigger of crazy power
   mongers with loaded weapons
Hear my gasp of disbelief and my calling out to
   stop the madness
   to stop the craziness in our world and this
   injustice

Hear me Mother
Hear me Father
Hear my plea for the innocent, brokenhearted,
   disenfranchised humanity
   that power be held accountable

Power Over
Over Powered
Power Hungry
Power Seekers
Power Mongers
Power Players

Power Power Power

Power in the hands of the
  unjust
  insecure
  undeveloped
  unskilled
  uninitiated
  un-empowered man or woman
  who gain a false sense of power by holding a
  gun on an innocent man, woman, or child
  so they can feel the wave of power
  he or she does not feel in everyday life

Forgive them for they know not
They know not that their source of power comes
  from within
From having a compassionate heart
From a discerning mind
They are possessed by their Fear, Insecurity, and
  the Hate that brews in their hearts
They will pay the price of the greediness for
  power
They will be forever branded as child killers and
  their souls
  will bear the mark of a killer of Innocent Ones,
  of God's Children

I would not want to be the one to bear that mark
Their shame will carry them onto the River Styx
   feeling the deplorable shame a killer of life may
   feel
This will be their burden to bear, their Karma to
   pay
May they be the lesson to others that those
   uninitiated into power
   are bound to use it as life-killing, death-wielding
   abomination of the use of power that it is

Real Power is life-affirming
Real Warriors discern if it is necessary
Where are the real Warriors?
I know you are out there
Please speak up
Please step forward
Please teach the way of the Warrior
   who is always in service to the good of humanity

Killing children is never in service to humanity
Killing innocent women is never in service to
   humanity
Killing men who are un-empowered is never in
   service to humanity

True Mature Discerning Men and Women of Power
   never kill unnecessarily and will look for ways

to avoid taking a life
I honor these Warriors of life
We know them
We've been protected by them
We've been blessed by them
We've been married to them
We've been born to them
We've had them as Fathers Sons Brothers and
Husbands
Mothers Daughters Sisters and Wives

I call on the honorable to stand up
and be the force of nature you are
for the good of the world
Would you please stand up for what is right and
just?
Killing a six-year-old boy in a spray of bullets is
never okay

Blessings

My Mother
My Daughter

My Beloved
My Precious

My Guiding Light
My Night Star Child

My Purpose
My Passion

My Truth
My Light

My Salvation
My Prayer

My Grace
My Devotee

My Hope
My Resurrection

My Mystical
My Magic

My Blessing
My Amen

The Foretelling

What is this?
I am no longer a daughter
I am no longer a little girl
I am alone

I have lost my daughter
I have lost my innocence
I have lost my little girl

I've been tempered, tested and tried
I feel deep powerful no-holds-barred wisdom
  kind of power

Deep abiding wicked wisdom
The kind that knows without saying
Speaks without compliance
Trusts the map of her own inner terrain
Travels the wild journey of change
Bucking the winds
Riding the waves
Surveying the horizon
All the while trusting the intuitive inner compass
  that has been long fought for over a lifetime

The adventure is just beginning
The terror is just beneath the surface

The hope shines brightly
And the fear niggles from the behind of my truth
Weathering the storm
Casting the anchor out and in, so I may land for
    this unknown moment
This is the unknown moment in this life of no
    longer being my Mother's daughter
    Alone, adrift, agog at the ever-changing
    landscape known as my life

I've never been here before
Quietly, numinously alone
Not terrified! Oh no!
But arms wide open, receiving the full grace of
    my wild nature
Wild
Wicked
Wiley
Wise
Wrecked
Wretched
Wonderful
Woman that I am
In this space, this place, at the sacred crossroads
    of my human and divine nature
Do I sell my soul to the devil for a turn at
    eternity?

Or do I revel in the Crone nature who lives fully,
  unapologetically, and
  unabashedly from her complete nature?

Oh! Me thinks, the wild wise Crone is the only
  way to go
Powerhouse full of purpose, pleasure, and pizazz
Oh my! The only way to go!
Selling my soul to the Divine image of Goddess
  and God
Accessing all that is God-Given in me

It is no longer my birthright
It is my life right
I have sown the seeds
I have learned the lessons
I have slayed the dragons
I have died and been reborn
I have been humbled to my knees
I have surrendered my desires
I have learned to listen to my intuition after
  suffering the consequences of not
I have fought the battles
I have tended the sick and dying
I have smelled the sweet scent of a rose in bloom
I have had great sex and indulged in good food
  and wine

I have been loved deeply and very, very well
I know the drill
I covet peace
I love unconditionally
I pray for Love to conquer all
I don't pretend to be something I'm not
I bless when I can
I forgive when it would be easier to carry hate in
   my heart
I love to the best of my ability

All of these things have
Scarred me
Trampled me
Changed me from what I thought I was to who I
   actually am

I am the wisdom that flows in my bloodstream
That comes from every breath I take
That creates from the spark of divinity mirrored
   to me in my Mother's Eyes
    and the eyes of those I love and care for

Wisdom is my name and
Living is my game!

Divine Mother's Blessing

Sweet love serenading your heart
Deep love diving into your soul
Abiding love opening into spirit
My love enveloping you this day
Beautiful love blessing you in this morning's
awakening
Devoted love in service to my daughter

Life's Blood

My goddess my heart
Feels like electricity
Ecstatic current

Prayer Flags

Sweetly delightful
Diamond hearts praising glory
Essence unfurling

Goddess Bless

Blessed is the Holy Child
That lives among you
Blessed is the Holy Spark
That lives within you
Blessed is the Holy Spirit
That is you

My daughters
My sisters
My mothers
My devotees
Transform your hearts
To love more richly
Transform your mind
To know more truth
Transform your bodies
To receive more love
Transform your spirits
To manifest more beauty

Goddess gives
Goddess receives
Goddess speaks
Goddess trusts
Goddess loves
Goddess protects

Goddess manifests
Goddess creates
Goddess blesses

Goddess is the reflection of your beautiful soul
Back to you in all its facets and dimensions
You are called to the mystical transformation of
    your being here on Earth
You are called to manifest your true light and
    shine it into the world
to lighten the darkened places
to illuminate the shadows
to bring forth that which is hidden in the world and
to bear witness to the holiness abounding within

Goddess Bless
Your beautiful souls
Your human selves
Your spirit incarnate
And your holy flame
Let it burn brightly in your heart of hearts

You my daughters are
The Mystery made manifest
The Holy in the hallowed
The Spirit in the flesh
The Great Mother
The Devoted Daughter

The Sweet Sister
The Blessing here on Earth

And I thank you

The Vital Mother

We are vital
Even when our strength and our work are
  invisible, it is still vital
We are vital
It is vital that we honor our effort, our essence
  and our bringing it into fruition

The Great Mother,
      The Divine Feminine is not docile or tame
She is the brave action
      The unpopular truth spoken aloud
She is the power enacted
      From a place of wisdom
She is the voice of love
      In the unloved
She is the faith in the intuitive hit
      In our heart of hearts
She is the guiding light
       On the path of chaos
She is the bearer of peace
      And the balance of power
She is the creatrix in whom
      All life springs anew
The Divine Feminine seeks a place
      In our hearts, our actions, and our world

She is the coming of Peace, Balance, and Justice
    The Way of Wisdom
Wage Peace
    Find your Sacred Roar
Reclaim the inner truth that you are
    Love and Light
    Power and Compassion
    Mirth and Reverence
    Strength and Wisdom
As we travel through the chaos of change
    We are the instruments of peacemaking
If we can tame the Devils within
    We can tame the Devils without
We have a sacred duty to Know Thy Self
    Know our divine origins
    Know our truth
    Know our light
    Know our power
    Know our place in the world
Amen

Answer the Damn Call

The call
What calls
Who calls
We call
They call
Calls from where
Calls what

The call
Calling up
Calling forth
Calling to
Calling from
Calling with

What are we to do
With the call
Answer it
Ignore it
Delve into it
Raise it up
Take it in
Brandish it
Banish it
Welcome it
Embrace it

The call
Calling up
Calling forth
Calling to
Calling from
Calling with

What happens when we answer the call?
Do we get heard or chastised?
Do we get blessed or broken?
Do we get dismissed or listened to?
Or do we get ignored and minimized?
Do we get shut out or shut up?
Or do we get championed and cheered?

It depends on what you ask
How fierce does the fire roar in your heart?
How fierce does the love fan the flames?
How fierce is your truth and will it ignite the fire?
How fierce is your commitment to healing the
    wounds of your foremothers?
Will it blaze like a roaring bonfire lighting the
    way for those to come?

Answer the call! Damn it!

The tsunami of flames of the fierce loving truth-
    telling conjuring creators

Will sweep you up in the wave of fierceness and
    carry you along
Until you can join your spark to the fire of
    transformation
Where the fierce flames of love will envelop you

Come on join the Revolution of Love!
It's your time
It's your gift
It's your lineage
It's your flame of love

Call yourself
Call your friends
Call your Mothers
Your Sisters Your Daughters
Your Sons Your Brothers
Your Fathers

Call everyone and all
To the fire
To add their spark
To the bonfire of love

Where we are the light of the world
Holding the fire for love, my dears
Hold it high for all to see
To let them know

It is always, yes, always
Always and forever lit!
For everyone to find their way
When they are ready to answer the call!

Two

Peregrine

Wandering, traveling, seeking
on the sacred journey

Prayer to Our Mother

Dearest Earth Mother,
You, like all mothers, make sacrifices for us every
    day
Dearest Earth Mother, you provide for us every
    day
Sun and light nourish your life-giving body
You envelop all of us in your mantle of love
All animal, plant, mineral, and human find
    nourishment at your table

You bless us with your wind, for it is our breath
Your water is our life
Your soil is our sustenance
Your spirit sings us alive in the thunder and
    lightning storm of a summer rain
Your moonlit sky provides solace and direction
    when we need to find our way

Mother Earth,
You have taken care of us forever
Let us send these prayers of love, gratitude, and
    peace to you, Dear Mother
That they may heal what ails you,
That they may bless and provide sustenance to
    you
As you have done for us for millennium

Let our petitions provide the strength for all
   creatures to bow in reverence to you
And act in a way that is respectful as you so
   deserve

Your seasons
Your cycles
Your beauty
Reside within us all
Let us return to you in gratitude
That same devotion to life as you have provided
   for us

May we bless you
May we honor you
May we love you
May we provide for you
May we serve you
May we shout out in joy for you
May we shower you with grace
May we open to peace and return peace to you

Blessed Earth Mother,
May we thank you with our tears of gratitude
May we thank you with our acts of devotion to
   you
May we thank you with our reverence for you
For all that you are and all that you provide
Now and forever
Amen

The Spring Equinox

Hail to the opening of new life
The warming of the days
The lengthening of light
The shortening of the night

Hail to the opening of fresh perspectives, budding
   truths
And the pushing through of our flowering
   essence

Hail to the clearing away of winter's solitude
And the stepping into the connection to new life
Within and all around us

Bless us in the turn of the season
May we remember our own freshness and beauty
May we tend to it and shelter it as it begins this
   new cycle of growth
Blessings to our emerging beauty

Here Is What I Know Today

The sun is shining, the snow is sparkling
And life has a way of being illuminated after a
  stormy time

The sun always shines again
The birds always sing in the spring
The water always thaws after a freeze
The blue skies always emerge from the storm's
  clouds
The heart always mends after it has been broken
The mind always grasps new perspectives when
  old ones have been shattered
The body always miraculously heals after a
  wound has been tended
And the beauty of a place always returns after a
  storm has wreaked havoc

We are resilient like the sun coming up at the
  break of dawn
We are resilient like the crocus peeking through
  the spring snowfall
We are resilient like the wonderful rainbow that
  appears in the sky
After a big summer rainstorm
That is how constant and beautiful our human
  spirit is
We are a force of nature, just like the ever-present
  constants of Mother Nature

Spiritual Ta-dahs

Innocence lost
Sadness revealed
Cumulative exhaustion
Raw spirituality
Reverent humanness
Delving duplicity
Wicked wisdom
Loving ancestors
Mother holiness
Thou art
She is
We are
Blind faith
Tempered soul
Tattered senses
Sweet remembrance
Tickled pink
Untold toil
Incensed solitude
Spoiled rotten
Wild thing
Sacred prayer
Spoken truth
Silly girl
Wonder woman
Wise sage

Hurry up
Hang on
Penetrating presence
Thou art
Moon Mother
Soul Sister
Divine Child
We be
Scoo-be-do-be-do-be-do
Amen alleluia
Praise be
Yahoo yippee
Holy Mother of God
Bless me
Thank my lucky stars
God's speed
Amen Sistah

The Way to Grace

Dear child of mine
Strife is the melody by which songs are sung
Challenge is the way by which a map is drawn
Sorrow is the way of sweet being sewn
Death is the way of new life awakening
Disappointment makes way for hurts to heal
Sadness is the precursor to love's gentle touch
Surrender is the bow to the revered holy
Release is the summoning of soulful
    remembrance
Tattered is the temperance of the teardrops of
    truth
Separation is the union of heart's glory
Disillusioned is the remembrance of spirit-
    sourcing self
Diving deep into the human frailties is the way
To the light-bearers of freedom's ring
Pearls are made from dark and compressed grains
    of sand
Grace is made from compressed humanity

The Ghostly Lover

Growing into my unlived life
Growing pains

I've lost my way to
The ambition of living
The seduction of success
The glimmer of being needed
The excitement of newness
The reflection in the mirror of giving and doing
The hallowed halls of productivity

I have lost my way
I have lost my vividness in the dizziness of my
    mind turning and spinning around
    in the tumult of these creative times
I have lost my sacred to the invitations to show
    up, be big, be bigger, do more,
    be more, live my passion, do epic shit, go big or
    go home
I have lost my soul to the "Isn't this great,"
    "We don't have much time left,"
    "Better make hay while the gettin's good,"
    "Be all you can be"
I've lost my spirit to the "Puella Aeterna,"
    the flying girl, flying high into the sky

Ever so high, without regard to her wings being
   burnt to a crisp
   from getting too close to the sun
I've lost my ground, my deep faith in me, the
   Mother's Blessing,
   and the ever deepening connection to my
   instinct and my wisdom

"How," you say, "Did you lose something so
   precious?"
Well, I lost it in the whirl and twirl of dancing
   with the ghostly lover Ambition
Who commands all my attention just to keep in
   step with him
As he stands still, in the wicked dance of
   deception, demanding my all
Be all
To all
For all
Forever
That's the dance of DEATH

Death of my soul, my spirit, my wisdom, my
   ground, my sacred, my vivid
Dancing me until I am nothing but skeletal bones
   clanging and clanking
As he captures me in his spell of seduction,
   wrapping his skeletal arms around me

as he swirls me and twirls me again and again
I am vaguely aware as he makes his last dip with
   me that my life force
   is slowly being depleted from me one dip and
   twirl at a time

It's an epidemic of doing
To fill the hole inside where insecurity and
   unholiness cackle in delight
To meet the demands of unrelenting standards
   and perfection-barking orders
It is mass hysteria (of the masculine principle) in
   motion
Because we drank the potion that cast a spell over
   us
   that we have to be big and do big all the time to
   be a good being

We break that spell by knowing that the grounded
   holiness of the feminine
   conjuring up the magic of our truth is what
   makes us whole and holy
   just by being ourselves

Thank you, Magic Mystical Mother, for saving me
   and conjuring me alive again
Amen, or rather Awomen, to the Divine Feminine
   who can kick butt

and take names with just a wink of her eye and
a tiny nod of acknowledgment
Letting me know that it's time to walk away
Before I am lost forever to the seductive,
spellbinding Ghostly Lover
and end up dying the slow death of depletion

"It's time," she says.
"Come home."

I Lost My Mojo

I miss delight
I think I worked it right out of my being
I miss love
I wish for love in my heart,
Along with peace, and energy, and excitement,
  and aliveness

I miss joy
Where did my joy go?
I miss my brilliance
It has been tarnished because of not listening to
  my body's wisdom
I've lost my mojo!

It's been misplaced, forgotten, misaligned, and
  lost once again
It happens to the best of us when life calls for
  more of us than we have to give
I lost my mojo!

It's been lost in the push, pull, and drag of my
  own unrelenting expectations
Lost in the depths of doing
Lost in the tired body
Lost to the have-to's
Lost to the get-it-done's

Lost to the giving too much to others
Lost to achievements and ambition
Lost to the day of work
Lost to the muscle-it-up
Lost to the fame and fortune
Although there is none to speak of except
    goodwill to the world

Amen to listening to the wisdom of the body
Where we all will find our mojo and our sparkling
    brilliant essence
Always and forever recoverable from the depths
    of our disconnected selves
In the quiet of any moment

Oh, I gotta go—I hear my mojo calling!

Wicked Rebel Poet

Wicked Rebel Poet
Sing your rebel song
Raw sweet sensual ballad of the heart

Dance your rebel dance in the firelight flames of
    creation
Sparkling embers flying all around you
Invoke the heavens with your incantations and
    spells
Calling forth beautiful rich ancient soul rhythmic
    chants

Dance sweet gypsy soul
Dance and revel and reveal your starlit essence
In your round and round whirling dervish
    feminine swirls and twirls
Open your arms and receive the Divine

Abracadabra
Amen
Wicked Rebel Poet
Bam!

Dance On

Dance on sweet sister of the courageous-hearted
Dance on through the toil and trouble created
  by the manmade patriarchy of hate and
  disparaging words
Dance on through the physical torment inflicted
  upon those
  who choose to speak aloud the atrocities done to
  them
Dance on through the clearly drawn lines of
  power
  that have been drawn to keep you below the
  acceptable levels of living forever
Dance on through the crowds of rock throwers,
  pyre builders, emotional terrorists, physical
  batterers, and spiritual destroyers of the feminine
Dance on to the heart of it all

We are the power sources of our time
  and we are dancing and gathering and holding
  this power
  to wreak havoc on your old power-co-opting
  ways

We are here to dance on the grave of the
  patriarchy of old
  and to gather and mind the both-and of
  feminine and masculine

Crush the regime with love that thinks women
and girls are objects
to be used and abused for sex, for play, for
power

We dance on your graves, your pinnacle of power,
your banks of money, your companies, your
hate-filled hearts
and dance and dance until life comes alive in
you again
Until you honor the Love of your Mother in your
hearts
and weep with recognition that she has always
been there
for you, with you, in you, and you were too
hate-filled to recognize her

As you weep with sorrow at the loss you inflicted
on others
the withholding of life-giving necessities from
deserving men, women,
and children out of your fear-filled heart

As you weep with regret that your heart was as
neglected as those
to whom you consciously created neglect-filled
life circumstances
of poverty of epic proportions, emotionally and
physically abandoned
You will reap the consequences of such neglect!

As you weep with contrition deeply, regretfully,
  sorrowfully aware
  of your own shriveled heart and your
  purposeful ways
  trying to shrivel the hearts of others less
  fortunate than you
Who also happen to be different in shape and
  color and ethnicity
  and class and gender

As you weep with grief at the loss of your deeply
  embedded
Brick-and-mortar wall barrier meant to keep "the
  others" out
  now crumbling in front of your heart eyes
As you fearfully see we are all the same human
  beings
  with heart and flesh and blood and bones and
  fears and joys

You no longer can keep "the others" at bay
  and are called to see the oneness of humanity,
  fearful as it is
You better count your blessings that this sea of
  different "others"
  is much more forgiving and compassionate than
  you have ever been

As you weep, they envelop your fearful, terrified
   little heart in the sea of empathy
Knowing that you were held captive by your little
   ego-self who blustered
   and filibustered out of a deep-seated fear that
   you are not enough
And from this cruel-hearted ego you aren't
   enough
But humanity sees beyond that and commands
   and demands
   that you grow up into your man-woman heart
   now!

Betrayal

Betrayal of the senses
Betrayal of innate wisdom that lives in the
ancestry of our being

Betrayal of the natural native peoples
that have walked this earth walk

Betrayal of the love of Mother Earth
and the sweet shoulders we lay our heads upon

Betrayal of the rivers and lakes
the tears of the Mother flowing freely

Betrayal of the love of the pure of heart
who shall shine forth and inherit the heavens

Betrayal of friendship between the holy order
and the humanity of the everyday actions we take

Betrayal of our hearts and the purity of our souls
being contaminated with not caring

Betrayal for the heartfelt that they may survive
the slaughter and carry the truth to safety

Betrayal
      Betrayal
            Betrayal

It justifies the cruel-hearted senseless annihilation
of our native natural instinctual trust in ourselves

Betrayal kills the heartfelt and rams shock and
disbelief down our throats

Betrayal has us choking on our grief and
throwing up our sadness and wailing in despair
at the cruelty consciously bestowed upon us

Betrayal is the justified harm done to another
under the guise of righteousness and the power of
the fear that you are not enough

Betrayal has you and now will hunt you in your
sleeping consciousness with nightmares for the
rest of your life

Betrayal is the last harmful act you do to another
before you succumb to the death of your soul

Tattooed Tribute to the Broken Hearted

Hollowed-out heart trying to beat again
Loudly, powerfully, full of life-giving life blood

Yet the hollowed-out heart is working so hard
To fill itself after the harm done to it
Oh, hollowed-out, empty, bruised, and bleeding
  heart
What do you cry for?
What do you yearn for?
What do you need to fill the emptiness that
  pervades the core of your vessel?
What do you need to pump fully alive?

What did the world do to you to be so hollowed
  and torn asunder?

The world does what it does
It Hurts
  Disappoints
  Wounds

It Harms
  Harasses
  And Creates deep crevasses of disappointment

It Hates
  Humiliates
  And Scars the heart

It knocks you on your ass and pushes you down
Like a bully on the schoolyard, it keeps coming at
  you
When you think you can't take one more
  knockdown

Yes! Life is hard, tough, disappointing, often
  debilitating
And reminds us that
It demands payment for being here, yes, a toll
  must be paid
Yes, the toll of hard knocks!

Life becomes smoother after the toll is paid
Yes, then life becomes smoother
Freedom happens
Relief comes and we begin to breathe again
Breathing into the moment where disappointment
  disappears
Breathing into the moment where the pain
  subsides
Breathing into the moment where the hurt stops
Breathing into the moment where the harassment
  recedes

Breathe into the moment
Breathe into this moment
Breathe into the moment

Where the hollowed heart begins to open and feel
   the lightness of hope
Where the hollowed heart is tended to with the
   balm of healing as it is
   placed on the scars
These badges of honor
Where the hollowed heart remembers its origins
   and begins to feel plentiful with purpose
Where the hollowed heart allows the beauty of
   life to restore it to its fullness
Where the hollowed heart comes alive again and
   again and again

Recognizing it is meant to return, remember,
   redeem, and realize
   that no matter what life does to knock us down,
THIS HEART IS HERE TO LOVE!
This heart is here to love beyond measure
Yes, love beyond measure
   our tender, our vulnerable, our kind, our loving,
   our open hearts
May we choose the beauty of the scarred heart
   that is tattooed
   with life experience

Wear them well, these scars, these totems of
   triumph

I would rather be bruised and tattooed with life
   and the triumphant
   tragedies of living
Wearing these tattoos as tales to tell my
   young ones that I thrived
   and returned from the hollowed-hearted
   tragedies of life's
   knock-you-down moments

I am a proud member of the Scar Clan and
   this is a Tattooed Tribute to the Broken Hearted!

The Storm

We are the frontier
We are not the fringes
We are not the disenfranchised

We are the wisdom keepers, the shared seekers of
    truth and light and beauty
    that lives in the heart of all hearts
We are The Mothers, The Daughters, The Sisters,
    The Wives
We live in the earth-shaking, soul-quaking
    frontier of the cutting edge of being
We birth ourselves, each other, and goodness into
    the world

No wonder the old and outdated masculine
    regime wants to silence our efforts,
    our voices, our words, our truth, our demands
    for equality and justice for all

No Wonder! No Wonder! No Wonder!

The wonder has been abducted and turned into
    data
    that supports the power-hungry "power-over"
    culture

The wonder has been extracted one beautiful
    spirit-filled drop at a time
    from the soul of our souls to be replaced with
    hate-mongering and suffering

We women, we know about suffering
From birth to death, we endure the pain of it all!
We live through whatever is thrown our way
    and we don't allow it to steal our souls
We magically transform our suffering into badges
    of honor
    that we display over our hearts proudly

We take the suffering which is given to us
    and alchemically transform it into gold
    because we are the caregivers,
    the life sustainers,
    the nurturers,
    the nourishers of life

We are on the frontiers of the hateful
    carving out the path to love
With enough love hate turns from its cold-hearted
    frozen existence
    into transformed, heart-heated, warm love

We are on the frontier of new life
We take the deadened crusted-over

and scrape it off until we reveal new life
Then we tend it until it raises its shoots to the sky
  and is grounded in its life source

We women
We know suffering
We are the
Discriminated Against
Violated
Demeaned
Diminished
Devalued
Desecrated
Demonized and Killed
And we still keep coming
We keep coming to breathe new life into any and
  all willing to live on the frontier of creation and
  rebirthing

Just try, I dare you, to create as we do
You wouldn't last a day or an hour or a minute in
  the birthing pains of labor
No wonder you are so terrified of the Feminine,
  the Divine Feminine
  and the Earth-based Woman
No wonder you quake in your boots and try to
  silence and still
  any movement we have made

Because you know we are the storm coming!
We are coming to whisk away and to crash the
  waves of faith
  against the doctrines of the male religion
We are coming to erupt our power and blow the
  lid off the injustice
  done in the name of God
We are coming to twist the angry hate-filled
  vernacular
  and in one clean sweep make room for the
  language of love and belonging
We are coming to strike a lightning bolt of truth
  into the lies of the ages—
  that women are cursed!

We are miraculous!
We are coming!
We are the Storm!
We are going to electrify the atmosphere with
  hope and value and connection!

Yes, we are the game changers, the rule shakers,
  and soul makers
The power source that allows life to be lived well
With peace in our hearts and gratitude in our
  actions
  for all that we have been blessed with

We are coming to cast a wide net into the world
    for the people who choose love
    to gather together and craft, and blend, and
    carve, and weave,
    and stir, and plant, and harvest the truth

We Are Coming!

We Are The Storm Of Creation!

My Wish for All of You

Allow
Believe
Cherish
Delight
Enjoy
Forgive
Grow
Hope
Inspire
Joy
Kindle
Luxuriate
Mambo
Nurture
Optimize
Presence
Question
Revere
Savor
Treasure
Unite
Vision
Wonder
eXcite
Yearn
Zig Zag

Journey's End

Unsweetened savory
   Undone knots
      Undulating winds

Deep riches
   Mined gold
      Gems gleaming

Hollowed heart
   Broken open
      Unsettled truth

Mother's bearing
   Birthing death
      Defying ages

Brigit's candle
   Casting shadow
      Eternal flame

Journey's end!

Amen

Peace be with you
Love surround you
Blessings to you
Honor in you
Beloved in compassion
Dear One
Mother's Daughter
In heart, soul, and spirit

Three

Instatus Nascendi

Lifting the veil of survival
and mining for the jewels
hidden within

Diamond in the Rough

Half-crazed by union with the resurrected faith in
life
Dizzying with spirit twirling, whirling until I fall
and tumble into place
Whole-hearted amazement at the ground swell of
sweet surrender's message
Vision glimmering with starlight in holy
reverence's twinkling eyes
Totality tasting the lavish feast of the Universe's
bountiful love
Holy moly, the gift of dying is the early morning
refreshing awakenings of sun-kissed lips
The serendipitous trails lead the lost to the found
And to the most amazing treasures

Traveling inward, one must shed all the veils of
survival
And stand naked in love's embrace
Reveling in the sparkling of rubies and diamonds
and emeralds
Of our ever-faceted beauty
Sanctify your goodness with the water of life
And bathe in the delight of the Goddess's bubble
bath
Luxuriate in the ever-present as it surrounds all
the curves

And crevasses of your being
Sink deep into the warm, sweet-smelling waters
   of rejuvenation
And arise dripping with bejeweled water droplets
A newly Arisen Resurrected Resplendent
   Diamond in the rough

Divine Mother's Morning Talks

Exquisite

Given a moment
Blessings shower upon us
Essence revived

Strength of the Mother

Blessed be my love
Deep holding, deep peace my dear
Love surrounding you

Love's Embrace

Blessed be dear one
Holy holding of your vulnerability
Swept up in my arms

Spirit's Combination

Unraveling lock
Heart breaking, flames burning,
Soul enlivening me

Mystical Sisters

Veil lifting
Soul quenching
Heart abounding
Vulnerability opened
Courage availing
Beauty revealed
Sacred sealed
Treasures unveiled
Hope prevails
Lies broken
Truth spoken
Love heals
Power released
Tender nurturing
Sweet surrender
Essence ignited
Transformation tended
Souls mended
Gold poured
Restoring reverence
Wabi Sabi wisdom
Original face
Delicious delight
Spirit raising
World changing
Fierce feminine

Wonder women
Heart warriors
Soror sisters

Vastness

Dear child
Feel the vastness in your heart
The vastness of eternity that leads you to the truth
  of who you are
The veil dropping off
One veil at a time revealing the deep truth of your
  essence
Free from the shackles of the prison
From past sins perpetrated on you
Free to sing the note long and strong
That is yours to cry out and hold as long
  as you like
Free to open the closed door to the vastness of the
  night's starlit sky
Free to be the hallowed holy light that radiates
  from your core
And lights up the beauty of the sun-revealing day

The Sins of Eve

It's tough carrying the sins of Eve
It's tough being a woman who is sin, sinned upon
Wreaks of sin, punished for the sins of being
  a woman
A woman with a scarlet letter sewn onto the skin
  of her chest
Where it is worn as a flashing beacon
Telling the world
You were born of sin
Sins of the father
Bestowed upon you
Perpetrated on you
Assigned to you
Sins for being a female child
A sin for being a child-carrying woman
A sin for laughing too loud, standing too tall,
  speaking truth too directly
A sin for carrying power in your body, your mind,
  your words
A sin for being, yes being, the receptive, the
  creative, the bleeding
A sin for being, yes being, the caregiver, the
  container, the nurturer
A sin for being, yes being, the sensual, the sexual,
  the sincere

A sin for being, yes being, the smart, the serious,
  the sunshine
A sin for being, yes being, the warrior, the wild,
  the wizened
A sin for being, yes being, the gorgeous, the
  powerful, the precious
A sin for being, yes being, the complete, the
  whole, the holy
A sin for being, yes being, the mother, the
  daughter, the sister
A sin for being, yes being, the sweet, the sorrow,
  the spirit

It's tough carrying the sins of Eve
Silence is the sister of sin
She is complicit in the act of sin against the holy
  you
Break the lock on your lips and speak
Break the spell that's been cast and see
Break the hold that bars your freedom and walk
  on
Break the chains of history and claim the truth
Break the lineage of fear and fill your heart with
  courage
Break the bindings of sins that have been spun on
  you
And flex your truth

It's tough carrying the sins of Eve
Of the culture against women
Against women's
Wisdom
Softness
Power
Purity
Strength
Stamina
Courage
Love
Nurturing
Creativity
Passion
Against women's bodies, minds, hearts, and souls
Against women's spirit

It's tough carrying the sins of Eve
Being a female child born in this culture
With a sin already marked on you identifying you
    as flawed
Men's fear of women frightens them to the core
Therefore kill them
Kill the female spirit
That's the intent

It's tough carrying the sins of Eve
The beauty of Eve as the mother of us all

Is that she has been branded, banished, berated, beaten
And misaligned from the earliest of times
Yet, yet, she was the way-shower
She was the wisdom seeker
She was the first, the brave one to seek consciousness
She is the creator
She has the ability to birth consciousness and babies into the world
She has carried the weight of others' fears of her for centuries
She is the carrier of the sins of others
Like Kwan Yin, she doesn't want to leave until all beings are enlightened

It's tough carrying the sins of Eve
For the compassion of the open-hearted, woman-Bodhisattvas
Will bring the light of the Mother to the sins of the Father
And cleanse the heart of sin until it bleeds light

It's tough carrying the sins of Eve
Yet there is no other purpose for me
Than to do her work here on Earth
Love the sins and sinners to death
Be a card-carrying bearer of the sins of Eve

Transforming the sins of the sinner one at a time
Through the Feminine's saving grace
Which is Love
Love our humanity and transform the tough into
the treasured

Awomen

Silence I

Silence is golden
Seek silence in the emptiness
In the soul and be free
Except when Silence is full of shame

The shame of
You are dirty, disgusting, something-is-wrong-
  with-you
You are defective
You are the cause of the dirty disgusting fear and
  defective badness in you

You have been marked with original sin
You are the sin
You are the girl
You caused the perpetration
You had the sin in you at the tender age of six

Everyone will see the sin in your eyes
You are the consent of sin upon you because you
  were indoctrinated
To play nice
To be a good girl
To not inconvenience another by telling the truth
To not be a burden
To not hate men

You have four brothers and a dad
Don't cause trouble
Don't wreck another's life

Be silent
Carry the shame the male babysitters
Yes, sitters plural, branded you as a six-year-old
Terrified, confused, shame-filled, dirty feeling
Did I say this is how the innocent little girl felt?
As the male babysitters wounded your little soul
    to the core?

Leaving a scar-tissued, jagged reminder that you
    are marked
As a scarlet-letter-carrying, sin-filled, abandoned
    God's child
Left to the dark, slimy, defective, dirty shame
That was departed on you and imprinted in your
    pure little soul
A card-carrying, shame-filled, silenced female
    child

Silence killed my innocence
Silence protected me
Silence perpetuated the abuse
Silence is a death sentence
Silence is a lifesaver

Silence co-opted my soul
Silence is the truth denier
Silence kept me a prisoner
Silence set me free
Silence cauterized my scars

Silence sealed the shame in my body
Silence made me pretend it didn't happen
Silence kept me safe from judgment
Silence harmed my right to exist
Silence broke my spirit

Silence captured my sexuality
Silence deadened my senses
Silence helped me leave my body escaping the
    horrid touch
Silence killed my authority
Silence raped me and penetrated me over and
    over and over again

Silence molested me and annihilated my
    preciousness
Silenced froze me in time
Silence created a heart-hollowed existence
Silence invented a panic room in my body
Silence taught me to rage inside these private
    quarters

Silence burned the coal of anger deep in my core
Silence prevented me from speaking out loud
Silence told me it was for my own good; do not
  speak of such things
So the tables can never be turned against me

Silence blamed a six-year-old girl for being the life
  wrecker
The cause of the destruction of a family
She couldn't stand the weight of that
  responsibility
And the fear that no one would believe her over
  the golden boys
Yes, plural, but not boys
Adolescent teenage young men who knew better
But did bad things to the little girl anyway

So she zipped her memories deep inside her mind
  and shut the door
Locked and threw away the key
To keep peace
To keep safe
To not bear the burden of being turned against
Because wasn't she to blame?
Because she felt so much shame?

Silence has proven to be the equalizer and the
  perpetrator

I grew despite of it and because of it
It cost me deeply
I spoke with victims because we were safe with
each other
And we needed to be believed
It helped me believe and fire shame as my
companion

Actually I had to kick shame's ass repeatedly
Because every time I confronted the untruth
Shame came back with a vengeance
With the age-old verbal abuses to silence me and
cover me
With shame and back me into the shame-corner
again

Silence doesn't hold the power any longer
It doesn't hold sway
It doesn't get to sit at my table feeding me ages
and ages
Of millennium old crap that silenced me for fifty-
two years
And women for centuries

Silence is not my keeper any longer
I am not imprisoned
I am not Silence's prisoner any longer

I break the silence like a sledge hammer hitting an
    anvil
Hard repeated blows breaking the chains into
    shreds and tiny pieces
The iron clad dropping to the floor with one
    powerful blow at a time

Setting my innocence free, for I am not guilty
I am not a crime to be perpetrated on
I am free from shame's chains that have kept me
    locked in that tiny room

I am free as the door that was locked long ago is
    opened wide and
I walk over the threshold of shame and claim the
    key that is my birthright
I am free from the shame-penetrating-scarring
    abuse
That was branded on my body
I will no longer be Silence's whipping girl

Silence II

I am free free free
I am the strength in the warrior
I am the magic of the priestess
I am the love of the Divine Mother
I am the instinctual wisdom of an embodied
  woman

I am free!
I am free!
I am free!

Free to speak up, speak out, speak truth, speak
  my thoughts
Free from Silence's menacing glare
Free to look into the eyes of another and see my
  innocence reflected back at me
Free to be the essence I was meant to be
Broadcasting and blaring my vividly intense
  essence loudly

I don't regret the wound
I regret that Silence robbed me of my innocence
And gave me shame as my companion

The wound made me strong more than I ever
  thought I would be

It made me more conscious and capable
It made me more compassionate to the plight of
   others

And it made me wholly who I am today
Scars and all
Worn like badges of honor
For I belong to the courageous scar clan of women
Who have been silenced forever

I am free free free
Take that, Silence!
For I will have the last word and it is
"Let Freedom ring!"

Quiet Death

From Deathly Quiet the body hears the slow
  growth and regeneration of each cell
    turning life's blood over and over until new life
    awakens

From Deathly Quiet do you hear the bump bum
  bump bum of the beating heart
    rhythmically reminding me of the natural slow
    beat of the inner world

From Deathly Quiet does the mind open and pour
  forth images of light and dark
    solace and silence inviting slow-rolling beauty
    through its doors

From Deathly Quiet the sensual siren sings her
  song of longing for wisdom's
    instinct to return to the right hand of her throne

From Deathly Quiet the beauty of spirit enters
  and awakens me to the brilliance
    of the ruby red sun lighting the path home

From the Deathly Quiet
I sleep the sleep of the ancestors
  dancing dreams and visions of old

Ancient ones gathering in my soul
   with every step, stomping and stamping
   their truth into my being

From the Deathly Quiet
I hear the Holy One:
   "Only this alive moment matters"
   "Stay alive in every moment"
   "For this moment may be your last"
   "And would you have your last moment
   be filled with the emptiness of self and soul or
   would you rather know the taste of Divine upon
   your lips?"

Your choice in the Deathly Quiet is to live in the
   falling-into-your-soul
Bathing in the treasure of your spirit essence
Soaking in the rhythm of the soothing
   Deathly Quiet

Freedom's Child

Bestowed grace
Beloved granted
Purity's presence
Peaceful power
Glimmering jewels
Granted entrance
Courting beauty
Common purpose
Elegance perfected
Elixir poured
Delicious delight
Dancing dervish
Ecstatic motion
Essence magnificent
Stirring spirit
Salutations spoken
Bowing reverence
Blessed awe
God's prayer
Goddesses anointing
Inspired holiness
Incredible humanity
Freedom's child

Paradox

The calm before the storm of a new day dawning
The sweet before the surrender of my soul
The cherished before the kneeling down in
   numbness
The grace before the grit of living
The flight before the fall into redemption
The pleasure before the pain of the little death
The peace before the twilight of a new night
The flicker before the burst into flames of
   annihilation
The twinkle before the dark night descent
The rise before the fall from grace
The hope before the dissolution of me
The living before the dying ember

Be the Soul of Emptiness

Be the soul of emptiness
Allow the ocean of love
To wash it clean

Be the heart in renunciation
Allow the forgiven to be
Offered up for love's embrace

Be the grace in the grit
Allow the soul to awaken you
In the slumber of your sleepwalking ways

Be the paradox in the present
Allow the confusion to
Deepen your faith

Be the prayer in the love
Allow it to spur you on
In the death of this moment

Be the spark in the illumination
Allow it to burn down any illusions

Be the truth in the matter
Allow it to ground you in your soul

Light of My Life

What do you have for me today, dear Death
 Mother?

Death of the ugly separated heart
Death of the single-minded cruel critic
Death of the hollowed-out vessel of my body
Death of the alone lonely existence
Death of the swift reprimand of punishment
Death of the bent-over kneeling in remorse
Death of the silent fear stalking my soul
Death of the separated spirit by a million miles
 from my beloved
As in all deaths, there is a light that is snuffed out
 for a monumental moment Flickering out with
 that little puff of smoke
Rising, letting eternity ring loud in the silence of
 that exact moment
Feeling the weight of emptiness and yearning for
 the spark to ignite once more
Only to have the flickering and sputtering of the
 spark of fire take hold again
Lighting eternity's darkness once more with a
 single solitary flame of hope
Hope that the eternity of the emptiness in the
 darkness be kept at bay once more

Under the Spell of Ambition

Ambition puts the weary and bone-tired into our
   everyday
Ambition steals the meander out of any journey
Ambition hurries you along as you attempt to
   smell the roses

Ambition is the purveyor of busy busy busy and
   seldom lets the sun shine down upon your
   upturned face
Ambition is the silencer of songs being sung in
   your car at the top of your lungs

Ambition is the squeeze-the-joy-and-life-out-of-
   you with its must-do lists
Ambition is the seductive siren calling to do all
   you can at whatever price
 for the promise of fortune and fame

Ambition is the bell tolling, reminding you to
   hurry hurry hurry
 for time is not your friend
Ambition lurks in the shadows, watching and
   waiting for the moment
   to snatch you away from the beauty of the day

Ambition is the societal measure of what is good
   and right
If there's something wrong, work your way
   through it
If there's confusion, work your way out of it
If there's fear, conquer it with hard work
If there's love, who cares?
Because work is what provides whatever you will
   need

Ambition caresses the wounds and puts salve on
   them and says
   "Pick yourself up by the bootstraps and do what
   needs to be done"
Ambition invites you to the table for nourishment
   only after you have depleted your body and
   heart with everything that needs to be done

Ambition cracks the whip and lures you into a
   spell of celebrating
   being a human doing
Ambition lulls the creativity of spirit into a deep
   slumber
   like Snow White waiting to be awakened by the
   kiss of truth

Ambition calls out to get on board
Step it up, work hard, work harder, take
   responsibility

Because no one else is, you alone have to do it
You are responsible
Look for what needs to be done
Don't stand around and wait for someone to tell
   you what to do
Suck it up buttercup!

Work hard and you will
Be successful
Be valued
Be seen
Be acknowledged
Be depleted
Be drained
Be empty
Be clumsy
Be tearful
Be yearning
Be hollow inside
Be Ambition's bitch!

For without love and joy, Ambition is just a
   power-over, slave-driving,
   whip-cracking, soul-stealing, life-force-eating
   Vampire
Who slinks into the night of day and seduces you
   under the spell of the living dead

So Ambition, you are unmasked, revealed, sun
    shining on you
    to show you and to see who's behind the
    Wizard of Oz Wizard Machine
You are the source of wanting to be seen and
    loved and valued
You push me into the world, so I will have a basic
    core need met
    to be seen and loved, and now, as Dorothy said,
    "There's no place like home!"

Home in my heart is the warmth of love and joy
    that I am God's child
I don't have to seek it, I am it!
Bless your heart, Ambition!
I love you to the moon and back
For you have been the face shown to me
But underneath the have-to-do lists and
    whip-cracking
    is my sacred, vivid self who gets to be!

Fear

Fear: we all have it, we all know it, we all live
  with it
    unwittingly allowing it to be the captain of our
    ship
Fear manifests in deprivation

Fear comes like a thief in the night raiding our
  heart
    and plundering our treasures
Fear is the nocturnal critic whispering sweet
  "you are nothings" in your ear

Fear finds a place deep in the caves of our body
  and promises
    that the bogey man will show himself if you
    don't behave
Fear sits on the edges of consciousness, cheering
  ever so softly
    for a break in the game of shame

Fear settles in like an unwanted houseguest and
  sits at the head of the table
    expecting to be treated like royalty
Fear slinks in the shadows of our mind
  inviting us to expect that big bowl of
  disappointment

Fear is the companion of shame, bullying their
   way through our consciousness
      creating havoc in a peaceful exchange with a
      beloved
Fear reminds us we are vulnerable to judgment,
   criticism, humiliation, and
      demeaning dismissal every day of our lives

Fear is unresolved food, clothing, shelter needs,
   and the real and deep needs of
      safety and security being challenged every time
      we speak
Fear calls out the names of our desires—to be
   trusted, respected, valued, seen,
      heard, loved, listened to, treated fairly, and to
      belong—like a drill sergeant
      making ready to humiliate

Fear belays the birthright of peace, self-esteem,
   and self-love for another moment
      when it sinks its teeth into our psyche like an
      untamed feral dog biting us in its
      quick, fast, and shocking way
Fear rallies around our nervous system, firing
   neurons to make our adrenaline
      spike to make way for us to fight, flight, or freeze

Fear most often prefers us to freeze at the sight of
    it, so we can become its slave
Fear, Fear, Fear, when it goes untamed,
    unaddressed, un-soothed, it becomes
    the way of derision and division and slinks
    away in the shadows for cover
    not wanting to be exposed or seen for its own
    fear of discovery

Fear, Fear, Fear really, really, really needs to be
    seen, heard, and treated fairly
Fear really, really, really needs to be soothed and
    loved and calmed
    as the human body and system recalibrates its
    response to the demands on it

Love, yep Love, safely soothing, calming,
    centering Love ...
That's the key that opens the door and lets fear
    walk into the light of day
Revealing that bump in the night as the sun
    bumping into the horizon
    of the morning, bringing with it clarity,
    illumination, and relief

So Love your fear to death
Fear is the only thing that will die from too much
    Love

Love, Love, Love your fear until it turns into a soft
Mushy, plushy stuffed animal ... perhaps the Velveteen Rabbit?

For Love is the only thing that is real!

Let Love Reign!

What do you have for me today dear Death
    Mother?

I see the sorrow in the eyes of the heart that has
    been broken beyond measure
I see the hurt register and the confusion sweep in
To mask the ever-present heart breaking
I see the devastation wreak havoc on the hopes of
    the innocent one
That lives in each of us
I see the false bravado emerge on each face as
    protection from prying eyes
I see the shame engulf you as your mind works
    feverishly to do battle
With this mighty foe and sorceress
I see the tiny spark of a flame dwindling down to
    a barely there ember
I see the slump of your spirit being put in the
    corner again
To have to sit by the sidelines waiting for
    permission to come out again
But what I mostly see is the toll taken and your
    essence extracted
From your existence, one deadening drop at a
    time
I see the hollowed existence that the critic creates
    for you

I see the untruths spoken, the lies laid out, and
the ever-present emptiness
In your heart of hearts
I see joy wither and die
I see struggle become normal
I see your soul hoping
Your heart yearning
Your essence demanding that you turn from the
indentured slave
You have become to the critic master

So I beg you, turn away, turn to the truth, turn to
the dying ember
And blow it alive to a crackling fire, so pure
essence
Your birthright, your soul right, your divine right
May live a holy, sacred, essence-filled life
Enacting truth
Living essence
Spreading love within and throughout the world
This is your way
Your truth
Your light
To lay claim to the spiritual warrior that is
within you
Called to fight for your right to be love and to live
from love
Every moment of every day

This is our only hope to transform the world
So grab onto your flame and fan it
Until it burns like a bonfire blazing in the night
Illuminating your truth and beauty
For all to see and be warmed by its heat
So they may follow and create fires of Love
Throughout the world for all to be transformed by
Let Love Reign!

Love's Medicine

Love's sway love's surge
Love's embrace love's face
Love's blessing love's testing
Love's mist love's fragrance

Beauty is the scent of love
as it breaks open the human husk
to reveal the tender-hearted soul child

Love casts forth the light
to create and craft the soul
in the God-given image of your essence

Love mends the human and spirit together
that which is alive may create your birth

Love mends the human and spirit together
so that which is alive may create your birth

All Saints Day

I have a tonic for what ails you
I have a prayer for what brings you fear
I have a blessing for what is in your heart
I have a love that permeates all darkness
I have a sweet abiding joy that lives in the heart of
  all women here on Earth
I have a faith that sweeps the lands and
brings peace
I have a fire that burns ever so brightly for those
  that must find their way

Dear daughter,
Keep
Your faith strong
Your prayers fervent
Your heart full of love
Your mind open
Your presence full of love for all
Forgive them, for
They fear
They quake
They compare
They judge themselves
Therefore they judge others, all out of fear

Yes, my daughter,
Out of fear of
Not being enough
Not being seen
Not being heard
Not being felt
Not being valued and
Not being respected for who they are
We all know this, as we have all experienced it,
And we all are needed to heal it

Dear Daughter,
I will keep thee and my children safe as always
Awomen and Amen

Letter from the Mother

You were reborn of the Holy Spirit and fashioned
   through grace
In the image of the Divine
Your soul is your gift to the world
Live from it and receive the gifts of the Mother
Beautiful is the springtime of death and rebirth
And awakening and opening of yourself to the
   stirrings within
Feel the shedding!

My dear daughters, it is good and right this work
   we do
Clear
Cleanse
Reclaim the Instatus Nascendi
"The jewels hidden within matter"
You are to free the beauty in you
It is to be birthed and claimed and lived into
Death and Resurrection
Rebirth and Fruition

My Children My Daughters
Blessed be you
I see your gifts
I see your commitment
I see your truth spoken

I see your heart broken
I see your eyes opened
I see your sight restored

You know the wisdom in your soul and in the
    bones of your being
The light that shines in you shines with my light
No more walking in the shadows
No more walking in the dark

No More! No More! No More!

Light the way
    So others may see
Light the way
    So others may follow
Light the way
    So others may awaken to their inner beauty
    Their deepest capacity
    Their divine design

Light the way
So love and trust and faith
Become the light upon the darkened road
Become the light that illuminates the day
Become the light that shines forth from your eyes
And grants grace upon those who do not see
    their own

So it becomes the Compassionate Light of Love
That heals the discord
That heals the downtrodden
That heals the heartbroken
That heals the sick and weary
That heals the arrogance of man

Become the one-of-a-kind
Uniquely you
Special beyond measure
Soulfully designed
Spiritually ordained you

You who shines from the beyond of your human
    conditioning
You who shines from the beyond of your false self
You who shines from the beyond of your split-off
    self
You who shines from the jewels of your true
    nature

Sparkling
Colorful
Unique beyond measure
Priceless
Treasured
Awe Striking

Inspiring
Divine
Beautiful
You
Shine brightly as the beacons of light and beauty
  that you are my daughters
Amen!

Four

Retrieving Our Inner Brilliance

Restoring our birthright, beauty and essence to its rightful place

Temenos

Sacred Space
Living Hope
Tremendous Spirit
Unfailing Strength
Flourishing Power
Sound Determination
Bejeweled Desire
Decadent Soul
Delirious Hope
Hankering Heart
Heaven Sent
Hell Bent
Serious Living
Ta Da Ta Da Ta Da
Do Be Do Be Do
Scintillating Charm
Quiet Purity
Reveling Senses
Inspiring Courage
Imbued Love
Rocking Reverence
Wild Wisdom
Magical Delight
Sacred Sight
Vivid Boldness
Craftily Deep

Stirring Beauty
Holy Hallelujah
Temenos
Sacred Space
Sacred Place
Sacred Life
Sacred Heart
Sacred   Sacred   Sacred

Wonder

Lovely Body Wisdom Abounds
Heart Sings Love Alive
Second Sight Intuition Whispers
Spirit Messages Guiding Light
Pure Peace Saves Delight
Mother Goddess Blesses All
Sister Power Rebels Dance
Sustaining Glory Reflecting Beauty
Amen Alleluia Heaven Sent

Awakening and Resurrection

Awakening and resurrection were the words
Appearing like stars in the night sky
Resurrecting my essence from the burned out
   ashes
Of the abuse of Silence

Resurrecting the annealed sculptures from the
   oven's heat
Having baked it to a strength and character
That red hot heat can only forge
The heat of the fire of transformation

Heat
    Hot
        Red
            Fire
               White
                  Pure
                     Flames

Swallowing the gem whole within the kiln of the
   heart
Forging beauty and essence into treasure

Molten
    Blown

Caressed
Sculpted

To represent the human essence forged from fire
Blown into existence by the breath of God

One of His Own

I have yearning and truth and love
Deep love from childhood that lives in my heart
I am
One of his own

Accepted
Seen
Valued
One of his own

Delighted in
Loved
Welcomed
One of his own

Embraced
Encouraged
Excited
One of his own

I feel the love of being one of his own
My Father
And The Divineness

Heaven Sent

The meeting of Heaven and Earth
In the poetic spoken aloud
It brings peace and groundedness together

Holding spirit and body so strongly and sweetly
Tenderly opening my heart and soul
To the music of my ancestors

Banging drums
Melodious flutes
Violins weeping
Chimes tinkling

All to play the music of my soul
All to bless the human suffering
And give voice like birdsong
In the morning sunrise to Joy's melody

All to open my eyes to the beauty of within
Like unmined diamonds peeking out of cave
    walls
Ready to be plucked and polished to a shine
Revealing a little piece of Heaven on Earth

The pressure of thousands of Earth years

Compressed into a little gem of Heaven's treasure
 sent
To allow us to be dazzled
By the God-sent radical gift of who we are

As unique and faceted as the diamond fashioned
From the coal of its Earth body
We are fashioned the same

So withstand the pressures of becoming
And you will pluck the diamond of your
Heaven-sent from your heart

Pluck your gift and sparkle away
In the light of the Divine
And rest in peace as the grounded
Earth-gift that you are

God's Grace

Angels weeping
Devils sleeping
God's twinkling eyes speaking of Love
Forever mirroring the beauty of your essence

Women praying
Men swaying
Goddess dancing alive the essence
Of each in every dip and twirl

Sun warming
Moon illuminating
Each of us walking in the shadows of
sparkling stars
Waiting for an audience with the Divine One

Men loving
Women laughing
United in union with the love of all loves
The sweet embracing Amen to the Alleluia

Glory Child

Freedom rings
Truth lives
Beauty abounds
Softness prevails
Heart opens
Soul sings
Spirit dancing
Sweet sounding
Sacred grounding
Vivid majesty
Divine feminine
Peace pilgrim
Fierce fire
Sweet reverence
Holy wisdom
Young heart
Old soul
Ecstatic prayer
Love shines
Delight bows
Silence applauds
Bold blessings
Pure gold

Fire Light

Resurrected out of the ashes of the house that
   shame built
Real alive transformed by the fire
The fire of transformation
The fiery hell leading to the light of the world
Revealing through the smoke and flames
   deep abiding beauty
Gleaming with the polish of a golden statue
Forged in the fire of resurrection and rebirth

Alleluia dear child of the Mother
My sacred child alive and well
Walking through the cleansing flames
Being washed of sin as water washes away
The grime and shame of Silence's spell

Fire is the transformational agent
Slowly burning one ember beneath the
   rubble of time
Waiting for the whisk of a breeze to stoke its
   flame
Igniting it until it is roaring leaping dancing
   destroying anything in its path

Fire
  Brand
      Blaze
           Behemoth
               Burning
                   Beauty

Fire
  Fierce
      Foe
           Feast
               Flame
                   Fear

Fire
  Ignite
      Raise
           Resurrect
               Wreaks
                   Mesmerizes

Fire
  True
      Rich
           Real
               Warm
                   Light

Fire
  Cleanses
      Clears
          Lives
              Dances
                  Destroys

Go into the fire
  Let it wash away
      The sins of another
          And cleanse the body
              Like a water-cleansing bath

Remove the grime the grit
  The soot
      The layers
          The residue of old

Resurrect the refreshed soul
  From the fires of life and anoint
      Your body with the holy fire
          Of illumination

Phoenix Rising

I came walking out of the
Flames of destruction
Hair on fire
Clothes singed
Blazing from the billowing smoking darkness
Striding forth
Emerging through the cloudy
Fire-whipping threshold

Burning the door to the locked inner room
To the ground
The key and lock melted
Into a liquid lump of gold
The dark hidden
Lit up on fire
Walls charred
Scorched remains of the enclosed panic room
Blackened with the burning of the prison

In the light of day
Revealing the dungeon of shame
Burned like a funeral pyre
Nothing but sweet ashes remain

Sifting through the aftermath of the torched room
For any remnants of innocence left behind

Standing, surveying the demolished ruins
Of an age-old structure
Scanning for signs of anything familiar
Tokens from a long-ago age
Nothing but burned-to-the-ground
Smoldering remnants
Of what used to be the house of shame

Now a Phoenix rising
Out of the ashes
Like a sun blazing
Spreading its wings
As the Universe opens
To the eternity
Of another day breaking

Rising strong ever-present
Powerful reminding
That love will always see above
And shine on the ruins of pain
That shame built
Love will always eternally rise
And shine its light brighter
After it has ignited and burned
To the ground the house
That shame built

Holy Child

My holy child
My freedom's child
My joy-filled child
My child playing in the streets without a care

Welcome to the world sweet one
Welcome to the world where you will be
Watched for, protected, and promised
The treasures of your birthright
Love
Trust
Strength
Goodness
Beauty

Holy moments ringing loudly
Holding the note until beauty hears the call to come
home
Until precious rings true and turns home from her
walkabout
Until innocence reveals herself from her hiding
place
And curiously steps closer to the sound of the
holy

Until sweetness perks up and twirls back in the
  direction of home
Until delight smiles broadly and takes a curtsy as
  she dances her way home
Until the little girl bows in reverence to the holy
  notes
Swinging wide open the doors of home

Until each treasure is returned to the treasure
  chest of your holy being
Sparkling brightly as the crown jewels of your
  truest self
Ever and always present and bright
Shine on sweet one shine on
Let the brilliance of who you are reflect your holy
  beauty into the world
Amen sweet one
Amen

Kicking Silence's Ass I

Kicking Silence's ass is not for the faint of heart!

I am not silent anymore
I will not be silenced anymore
I will not let silence threaten me anymore
I will not be abandoned by others' silence
    anymore
I will not keep silent at my table anymore

I will not
I will not
I will not

I will not be pressured into fear and silence
I will not go silently into the light of day with my
    head bowed down in shame
I will not be questioned why I am friends with
    people I don't know
I will not be perpetrated against by the very
    people who say they are here to help
I will not be made to feel that I did something
    wrong
I will not accept the invitation for self-doubt and
    question if or how I caused this

I did not cause someone to perpetrate a crime on
    me by being a woman
I did not cause this perpetration by answering my
    phone
I did not do anything to cause, deserve, invite, or
    encourage
    a sexual perpetration on me

Go to hell with the invitation to feel that I did
    something wrong
I did not!
I spoke up
I spoke out
I spoke for
I spoke because to not speak was to give
    permission for Silence
    to perpetuate the bad behavior done to others

I took a vow
I made a vow
  to my Self to never let Silence reign again
So the Universe said, "Let's see how serious you
    are!"
Will you fall into the comfortable denial
    and move into the next moment of the day
    and let silence bury the incident under a pile
    of other perpetrations you've endured?

Or will you bring this one to the forefront
　and attend to the violation
　　so it has a chance to be arrested and stopped
　　so no more will it be done on another woman

If you don't speak nothing will happen
#ME TOO
Speak up! This is your corrective experience
Stand in your truest self and lay claim to your
　truth and speak
　　because you can
　　because you're not afraid
　　because you have the groundswell of
　　competence to withstand
　　the questioning of your integrity as a person
　　and as a woman
And because you are committed to the protection
　of other women

Now that you speak the Universe is testing you
Are you really serious?
Can you really break the hold Silence has had on
　you?
Can you break the ancestral chains that have been
　wrapped around your mouth
Keeping you in fear and keeping you quiet?

The Universe says
Break the chains
Break the silence
Break the perpetration
Break the shame
Break the denial
Break the fear

Break Break Break

Open the manacles and walk out of them
   letting them drop where they are
Move out of the chains that bind you to Silence

Kicking Silence's Ass II

The Universe is providing
Release and contraction
Release and expansion
Release of the ancestry of Silence
Release of the embodied Fierce-loving Feminine

Release of the shame that binds me to the
   perpetrator
Release of the freedom that brings me alive in my
   truth
Release of my captivity from the dungeon of
   shame
Release of the deep honor and deep courageous
   integrity

Release of the shrinking from shame's glare
Release of the big empowered presence feeling
   body
   in every dark corner where shame has hidden
   cowering from sight
Release of stepping out into the light of the
   healing day
Release of navigating judgment's withering stare

Release of looking straight into the eyes of
   another with clarity

that I am and we are strong enough to withstand
the barrage of doubting interrogating questions
Release of standing firm, strong, clean, clear,
truth-filled

I am not to blame nor am I the crime
I have been victimized by another's historical
perpetration of and on women

No more will I stand in silence and allow Silence
to commandeer my truth
No more will my silence contribute to the silent
abuse of others
No More

I am not a little girl afraid of the abuse of disbelief
I am a kickass woman who will no longer tolerate
Silence's perpetration on me or any other

I understand the need for silence
I understand the need to remain silent
I understand that survival depends on silence
I just don't need to do silence anymore

So bam!
There you go Silence
Don't let the door hit you in the Ass on the way
out!

Wild Child Wonderment

What do you have for me today, dear Death
  Mother?

I have the wonderment of the wild one in you
The poema, the spirit in flight finding wings of
  love to free the numinous
I have the wild one ripping off clothes of
  constraint and living in the spirit of truth
I have the numinous presence lighting the fire
  within
So the needless and heedless can burn in the
  funeral pyre of love
I have sweet sonnets of love manifesting in the
  heart of all hearts
Bursting forth as a song bursts forth from the
  song bird of love
I have notorious lovers laying sway to the body
Bringing love alive like the well-played melody of
  a violin
I have union with the Beloved awakening the
  slumber of giants
Casting shadows here and there as shade for
  lovers to lie

That's what I have for you today dear wild child
  of mine!

Notorious

Whirl like a dervish
Surrounded by the pure essence of the divine
Sweep the threshold free of the yesterdays
And run wildly into today

Revel in the magic that is the dawning of your
    existence in this
Turning of one moment into the beauty of the
    one now moment

Cast your net wide in the open sky and lasso onto
    the tail of a cloud
And ride it until joy overtakes you

Succumb to the blasting of the horns of triumph
    and kneel in awe
As the heartstrings play that tear-spilling melody

Resurrect your lost soul and hold it up to the sun
Until it ignites into a blazing fire and lights your
    way home

Ecstatically dance your way through the streets of
    sorrow
And leave a trail of laughing truths
Like candy being tossed into the streets
Sweetening the day's moments

Arrive at your destination in exhausted ecstasy
Seating yourself at the Soul of your being
Ready to partake in the feast that is before you

Notorious, Oh Wanderer, Seeker, Traveler
I give thanks for our chance meeting
And your offering to drink this resplendent
Taste of the mystery

It is felicity flowing through me
Breaking me down into an ecstatic dancing prayer

Simple Truth

Love aligns in the weaving of your sacred
  tapestry
  where vivid is woven in the beautiful colors
  alive with love
This morning's hours reveal the most invisible to
  you

The deep heart talking
The spirit speaking to you
The soul making ground for you today
The deepness in your body craves the Mother's
  Blessing

The Mother's Blessing sweetens the heart and
  body
  and allows soul a place from which to gather
  you
  and keep you as you enter the day

Simple soulful sensual
  embodied Mother's Blessing is the ground from
  which I spring
  and return to moment after moment of my
  everyday

Tender mercy and grace
　　are what fill me from the blessing of our
　　Divine Mother
Sweetly calmly gently caressing me soothing me
　calling me home to my inner cathedral

Awe oneness reverence
　　fill me as I worship at the altar of quiet peaceful
　　rock of my ages
Divine Mother's sacred flames warming me with
　　the light of her presence
　　warming me from the inside out

Heart soul body
　radiating with her illuminating love
Sweet love is the heart of the matter in each of us

The Ma the Mat the Mater
　　the sacred ground from which I choose to walk
　　this day
With every step a burst of new life emerging from
　my footprints

　Filling and springing up wildflowers as Mother's
　　sweet reminder
　　that magic lives in every step we take into this
　　new day
We are the magic she has created from her sacred
　ground

Allow

What do you have for me today, Mercy and
  Grace?

Allow the truth
Let it break your heart wide open
Allow the beauty
Let it speak your soul's language of images
Allow goodness
Let it flow through you like a giant river with
  deep strong currents
Allow the God-given
Let it spring forth into the light of day as an
  offering to the world
Allow your heart song
Let it sing the essence of you alive in my
  every breath
Allow deep wisdom
Let it ring true in the body electric charging you
  with holiness
Allow grace
Let peace envelop your heart to your heart's
  content
Allow mercy's bow
Let it relieve your heartache and sorrow
Allow beams of joy
Let them radiate fullness from your holy origins

Allow the hope of all hopes
Let it ride the waves of despair
Allow generosity
Let it cleanse the palate of fear
Allow gratitude
Let it cast clarity and polish clean the mirror of
　any doubt
Allow sweetness
Let it soften the warrior stance and one-sighted
　stare
Allow your heart to beat with saving grace and let
　mercy hold you in abiding love
Let that be what you bring to the world today
Allow

Eternity's Promise

Sweet surrender to twilight's gleaming
A promise is made of a new day
every sunrise an awakening
to those who are brave
enough to open their eyes
to open their hearts
to wave hello and be greeted
by the promise of this new day
twinkling ever so sublimely
in the stars' last twinkle
in the fading night's sleep

A promise with every breath
of hope and beauty arriving
at the doorstep of your heart
waiting to be invited in
for morning tea

A promise with every listening
for the message of the day
that will hold you like an anchored ship
in the rising tides and crashing waves
that are part of the oceanic rhythms
of the every day

A promise with each mantra
chanted or spoken prayer
that the sweet Divine
will be your guide through
this day's complications
with curiosity as your compass

A promise with each
water droplet cleansing you
of your night visions
making way for the truth and beauty
of this new day dawning

With a promise
of the ever reverent request
for the Divine's blessing
to carry me home
when I get lost
in the day's distraction

With a promise to have
and to hold my most tender self
as the sacred sweet holy spark
that it is lovingly kindly protected
just as the goddess Brigit
tends her sacred flame

With the promise
for more breaths and chants
and messages and guidance
as the day diminishes
into the starlit night
promising again
the dawn and death of every day

With eternity exchanging night for day
and the promise renewed
as we awaken
from every night's slumber
anticipating the promise of each new day

Star Bright

Love surrounds you
Peace envelops you
Beauty enables you
Wisdom guides you
Alleluia sustains you
Amen creates you

Prayer is the way to the center
Of the Universe
It brings you home
To the Cosmos of your being
Connects you to the Universe
And its gifts
Allows the Divine to nestle
In your being

For a moment it feels like eternity
And mesmerizes the self
So the Soul can dance freely
So the heart can beat wildly
And the eyes can see clearly
So love glows brilliantly and
Tears can flow freely

From too much beauty being revealed
In a twinkle of the star in the night sky

Guiding us to our essence reverence
Where the Universe is being revealed
In that quick glimmer of twilight's stars

We but have to open our eyes
And be lost in the Universe and blink once
To be here and now in the presence of this day
Starlight star bright which star do I see tonight?
Mine and the Universe!

Brilliant Darkness

Brilliant darkness …
Softens My Soul
Heralds My Heart
To know that which is unknowable
Yet can be tasted with one whiff of recognition

Beauty lives in the quiet of the early morning
darkness
Where no light breaks into brilliant sparkles of
wisdom's presence
And knowing lives in each sparkling glimmer of
truth reflected in your eyes

Amen for being seen in the darkness

Amen for prayers being whispered in the quiet

Amen for the sweetness of Love
warming my heart with an inferno of
joyous delight

Amen for the sweet surrender of the
mind's chatter
revealing wisdom's treasured gold

Amen for Love's embrace that only the Divine
can wholeheartedly envelop me like a Mother's
protective loving cradle

Amen for the Alleluia of the sweet surrender of
the senses
and the beautiful songs of angels serenading the
dark into light

Amen Goddesses' and Gods' presence
for they bring aliveness to the death of each day

Amen
Amen
Amen

Peace

What do you have for me today, Dear Mother?
I have peace, dear child of mine

Peace to calm your heart
Peace to soothe your soul

Peace to love from
Peace to lead from

Peace to honor others
Peace to be of service

Peace to reflect in the world
Peace to bless in others

Peace to release into the hearts of men
Peace to invite into the hearts of women

Peace to run to
Peace to play with

Peace to covet
Peace to enjoy

Peace to relish
Peace to relax into

Peace to grace others with
Peace to grace your heart with

Peace my dear is the sought-after Holy Grail
Peace is the inner flame of trust and faith in
one's self
Peace comes after the long journey of the heart
Peace reflects the essential and true

Peace is lit from the inner flame of Love
transformed from human frailties
Peace comes from the hard work of remembering
who you are
God's and Goddess's child and creation
Peace reigns when Love sustains the broken bent
And belayed hearts of the weary

Peace Beloved Peace
She is the heart warrior
She is the compassion seeker
She is the empathy wizard
She is the sweet Love
She is the Mother of All

She is the hand out to raise lift steady calm
soothe remind
caress squeeze embrace gently hold and

encourage us to Love
each other as we would Love ourselves with the
beauty and grace
we would afford the Divine, for we are the
Divine's children

Peace Deep Peace to you

Presence

To be present is to be alive
To be alive is to be interwoven with life
To be interwoven is to experience the joys and
  sorrows of living

To experience the joys and sorrows
  one must put themselves in another's place,
  feeling their feelings,
  hearing their call for recognition and cries to be
  loved for who they are

One must open their eyes to see the thing in
  another
  that makes us alike in commonality, not derision
  or division

One must open their heart to the gift of love as
  well as the gift of loss,
  as both can bring us to our soul senses and drop
  us to our knees
  in reverence and awe to the raw beauty of who
  we are

One must choose, yes choose, to be an instrument,
  activist, pacifist, rebel,
  champion, challenger, or creator in each and
  every moment

One must choose to land in their truth and have
    faith in themselves
    and another, that we choose to be connected
    and complimented
    and compassionate as we walk this rocky and
    real life together

Presence
Presence Now
Presence Here
Presence to yourself
To another
To the challenge
To the easy
To the real
To the highs
To the lows
To the history
To the herstory
To the heavenly
To the hellish
To the benevolent
To the mundane
To the heart
To the soul
To the body
To the spirit

One must, we must, the world must savor the
breath of life and with
each savoring land in the rich and real beauty
that each breath gifts us with

Living this life, living our life, graced with,
blessed with this present moment
Where we get to honor the spirit of another, the
soul of another,
the unique beauty of another, the God-given of
another,
the birthright of another, the special unique
beyond measure genius of another
For when we honor another we honor our own

Presence
Your Presence
Is the healing balm
The saving grace and the savoring spirit
The manifest destiny of beauty
The real revolution

Your presence can lead the way, guide another
home, and create a revolution
of Love by landing with one breath, one look,
one connection, one presence

Yours

166

You are the revolutionary
You are the catalyst, the chrysalis, the crucible, the
  conscious creator
You are the evolutionary

All it takes to change the world is to be yourself
One breath at a time

We invite you, we encourage you, we implore
  you, we expect you
  to bring your ever beautiful, loving, brilliant
  presence into the world

Presence

Giddy Up Gorgeous

Inner Beauty owned
Outer Beauty dismissed

Betrayal of my Adorable
Betrayal of my Splendor

Dismissed Beauty
Disowned Beauty
Disavowed Beauty

Turn over the soul soil
For your forgotten Beauty
Sift and lift
Your Beauty up

Honor
Love
Nurture
Cherish

Love your Splendor
God's given gift
Of your Beauty

Remember the freedom
Of being unburdened
Beauty!

Beauty up sister!
It's going to be a
Glorious ride!

A Little Bit of Wild Wicked Whimsical Wisdom

A little bit of wild
A little bit of wicked
A little bit of wisdom

OH, who holds that little bit?
OH, who fans the spark into the flame?
OH, it is you, whimsical one

You, the one who lives in the darkness
Who whispers sweet promises into the wind
For us to hear the call

The call to deepen, to enliven, to enrich
Ourselves with the soul-truth spoken
Only in the darkest moment
You who gathers our secrets
And holds our hand in comfort
For we have lost our way

The who that chants holy words
Over our heads
Hoping the blessings will take root within

The who that rants and raves
At the stormy night asking for transformation
In the lightning and thunder of the night sky

The who that washes away
The dirt and grime of our wounded selves
That no longer serves our purpose

The who that anoints us ever so gently
With the sacred so we can
Remember our Divine origins

You are the who that shows up for any and all
    women
With a gentle touch and a sweet countenance
For the healing of the lost and left behind

You are the who that wears her bravery like a
    raven's shimmering cloak
Wrapped in black around her shoulders
Letting everyone know that your courage is hard
    won but there for each of us

You are the dark wild wickedly whimsical
    wisdom Mother
Always traveling the darkest path, sprinkling
    starlight
Illuminating the path for us to follow you home

Dearest Dark Night Mother
Thank you for your loving fierceness
Amen and deep bow to you
Black as Starlit Night Mother

Five

The Revolution
of Love

Embodying the Fierce Feminine
and her superpower of
"Love Always Love"

Doorway

Dervish literally means doorway

What doorway do you wish to travel through my
    dear daughter?
Is it the doorway of illusion or the doorway of
    love?

Doorways of illusion promise fame and fortune
Doorways of love promise your heart's desire

Your heart's desire lives in the wisdom of the ages
The wisdom of the ages lives in your instinctual
    rhythmic body

The ground of your being is the height of the
    starlit Galaxy
The starlit Galaxy lives in the twinkle of your eyes
    mirroring the beauty revealed with one glance
    upon your face

With one glance upon your face the doorway
    opens for the
    dervish to dance through to the center of the
    stunning Universe
The center of the stunning Universe is where your
    true beauty unfolds

like a red rose opening to the fullness of its
    blossoming soul

The fullness of its blossoming soul reveals the
    tender
    velvet to the touch petals of your face upturned
Your face upturned to the Sun's rays warming it
    with the heat
    of the Divine Mother's breath upon your brow

The Divine Mother's breath upon your brow, a
    kiss ever so gently
    anointing you with the sweet ever presence of
    love's embrace
In the sweet presence of love's embrace, dervishes
    dance through
    the doorway enveloped by the serenity of
    spirit's serendipity

Soror Mystica Blessing

I fell in love, I feel love, I see love, I teach love, I
create love, I preach love
My sanctuary is my circle of women gathered
together
To honor the sacred in themselves

They are the spirit incarnate
They mirror beauty in the midst of bleakness
They tend their weary souls with blessings and
patience
They walk the path bravely devoted to their own
growth
They sing songs of healing and soothe with their
sweet knowing
They revel in their authenticity and champion the
purist in each
They bless with a touching word or look of love

They worship at the altar of truth
And bow in reverence at the vulnerable in
another
They gather, tend, hold, and honor, all in the
name of love
Bringing themselves to the world as illuminated
lanterns of light

For the world to see beauty alive in their hearts
and actions

We are the devotees of Love
Love Love Love

Love creates and energizes the fabric of our being
We are beacons of Love,
mirroring Love for each other
To see how stunningly brilliant, sparkling,
beautiful,
and uniquely special we are
Love's brilliance
Shining brightly
For all the world to see

Soror Mystica Sisters
Brilliant beacons of light
Of love, of heart, of soul
Manifesting here on Earth
Illuminating the darkness with Love's light
Helping heal the world one brilliant
moment at a time!

Revolution of the Light Bearers of Love

Good morrow Dear Mother
Good morrow Dear Daughters and Sons
Good evening Dear Daughters and Sons and
  Sisters and Brothers
Let's start a revolution!
Your wish is my command!

We are the keepers of the light
The stokers of the fire of beauty
We light the soul afire for holiness to shine forth
From the depths of our eyes
In which to see beauty and goodness in the world

We are the blazing stars in the night sky
Offering constellations for direction
And guidance by the true North Star of Love
Shining down on us in every dark night of
  our existence

We are the holy illuminating moments
As the sunrise casts its ruby red morning blessing
  on us
Reminding us that we are the light that
  illuminates the day

We are the light that will warm the heart,
   imbue the body
And that will free the spirit

We are the light that will bathe and soothe
The weary, brokenhearted, disillusioned, and
   desperate

We are the light that will warm the cold-hearted
And bring peace and beauty to the upturned faces
That are looking for Love's embrace

We are the light that instills hope in our bodies
And calls for action for the good of each
And the good of all in our world

We are the light from which the Divine Feminine
   shines forth
Offering solace and guidance and blessings and
   courage

We are the light that honors the beautiful
   sparkling essence
That shines forth whenever we are called and
   invited
To be our full righteous powerful selves

We are the light that lives in the gleam of our eyes
After having an insight, an intuition, or an idea
That dances with and honors the creative spark
    within us

We are the light that is the fire of transformation
Turning the old into ashes, with flames licking the
    air with power and purpose
Generating for us and gathering to us our passion
    for truth and beauty

We are the light of the world holding
The lit lantern
The blazing torch
The gleaming beam for others to see and be seen
To honor and be honored
And guide and be guided
To gather and bless
And to hoot and holler
To comfort and caress
And hold and heal
To conjure and create
And sit and rest
To cook and clear
And stir and sparkle
To stoke and tend to the gathering soul seers in
    this world
For the Blessed Beloved to shine her ever-loving
    light upon us

May we be the Love we wish to see in the world
In every moment we can stoke that fire, we can
  sing it alive
We can dance with it or we can bow in reverence
  to it

Stand in the light dear ones
Radiate your magnificence into the world
Illuminate your world with your own unique
  brand of beauty
And cast a healing chant of love upon us!

I know you
I know your strength and reverence
For each other and the world
I know you will not now, not ever
Allow the light to be squashed out of you
For you are the Great Mother's Daughters and
  Sons
And Sisters and Brothers and her devout
  Devotees
And your lineage is to withstand any and all
  attempts
To squelch the light of love that is the holy among
  holies

We are the Light Bearers
Holding the Torch for Love

For all to see
For all to rally behind
For all to create from

We are the keepers of the Flame of Love
Keep your light alive
See it in each other and shine bright my dear ones

Shine bright!
Forever and always!
For we are the Revolution of Love!

Bless your hearts my Sisters and Brothers in
    Love and Light!
Go forth and illuminate the world with
    your brilliance!
The Great Mother

The Power of One

One word
One gesture
One glance
One act of kindness
One encouragement
One blessing
One acknowledgment

One turns into two
Connecting from this place
Of being seen
Of being respected
Of being treated fairly, kindly, loving,
   compassionately
Of being valued for who we each are
Human beings making our way in this world

The Power of One becomes the power of many
One voice turns into the rallying cry
  for equality for all and equanimity for many

One act turns into a movement for the good of
  each
  and the cry for acknowledgment of all beings as
  equal

One act turns into turning the tide of hate-
    mongering
    into the tsunami of the power of Love

One act turns one step into a million marching for
    justice for all

One act turns into voices raising into a chorus of
    righteousness
    calling for consciousness-raising consideration
    for all

One act turns into a sea of women and men
    standing united
    for the powers that be to acknowledge their
    rights as humans

One act turns into a powerful connection
    that has sent shockwaves through the world
That women and men will no longer tolerate
    being put upon, put down,
    erased, eradicated, raped, harassed, dismissed,
    demeaned, or put in our place

In one act we rise, we speak, we gather, we care
    for, we protect, we advocate,
    we organize, we champion, we nurture, we
    nourish, we change the way it has

been to the way it needs to be, caring for each
and all creatures on this planet

One Act

One
The power of one
You are the power
You have the power
You can use your power every minute of every
day to change the world

One
Immediately in this exact moment
You, yes you, can choose to empower yourself
And another human being with just one choice,
one decision

One
You are the One
You are the chosen One
You are the power of One
Your choice to be
Conscious
Kind
Compassionate
Considerate
Clear

Clean
Loving
Respectful
Valuing
Is the act that will change the world
You have the power
You are the power to change the entire world

For One can change the world of another
   with one smile, one look, one blessing, one
   kindness,
   one gesture of acknowledgment
And being seen as the human beings that we are
   does change the world!

The Power of One
Be the One

Be the One to lead the way, break the rules, to
   teach anew, to model truth

Be the One to stand up, stand in, stand for what is
   right and good

Be the One who sees beauty in another, who
   acknowledges, blesses, and cares for another

Be the One who stands strong, stands tall, speaks
   for, and protects the rights of others

Be the One who acts every day for goodness in
   the world, honoring love and beauty in yourself
   and in every other

Be the One to honor yourself so you can honor
   others in their "less than" with love and respect

Be the One to Bless, to be the change in the world

Be the One
You are the One
You Are One with the Divine
Make the Universe proud by exercising your
   Power of One
And be The Revolution of Love that "One" and a
   "Million" can be

One

Love

Dear daughter, I have Love for you today
Deep abiding, soul-reveling, spirit-dancing, heart-
  blowing
Mind-expanding, deepening into your body Love

Love is the answer to your prayers and the
  remedy for what ails you
The key to the magic door, the sacred text, and the
  language of the ancients
It is the light that illuminates the day, the
  darkness of the soul
And it is music to our ears

How can you Love? Who can you Love?
What can Love do to heal our broken anything?
Our mind, our heart, our body, our spirit
Love, my child, is the answer and the question

How does love heal? Well let me tell you how
  love heals!
It provides hope
It conjures up courage
It holds the tender
It protects the vulnerable
It is the catalyst for the alchemy of transformation
That changes cold-hearted fear into warm,

glowing, illuminating trust
It is the life force that awakens the deep design of
our destiny

Love
In love
Out of love
Because of love
True love
Rich love
Deep love
Loving soul
Loving heart
Loving hand
Loving hug
Loving gesture
Who loves?
We love
Our love
Be love
Abiding love
Gentle love
Fierce love
Tender love
Passionate love
Sweet love
Love Love Love

It is the transformative
It is the God-seed planted in each of us
Ready to be tended to, watered, and cared for

It is the life force
It is the heart-stretching, tear-streaming
Mirror of beauty that we all desire

We all need and want to see and feel Love

Bring Love, exchange Love, allow Love
Be the Love you wish to see in the world
Change the world by being your big, bold,
  bodacious Loving Self

Love is the revolution that changes the world
One exchange of Love can transform the world
Be the Love you wish to see in the world

Love
It does
It can
We do
We can
We be do be do be do be do

Amen
Alleluia

Deep Love
Deep Loving
Deep Love to you!

Fierce Feminine

It takes the Fierce Feminine in all her love and
mercy to see beyond
the hurt and fear to the brilliance of what we
each are

It takes the Fierce Feminine to set fire to the old
limiting beliefs
and transform them into the golden riches of
wisdom and truth

It takes the Fierce Feminine to be open and
to discern
that which makes each of us oh so human and oh
so brilliantly divine

It takes the Fierce Feminine to stir the pot of
creativity and patiently cook the ingredients of
beauty, slowly, steadily stirring until it's finished
into sustenance and nourishment for the soul

It takes the Fierce Feminine to rise like the
Phoenix
out of the ashes of subjugation and stand firm,
strong, tall
and empowered in the body wisdom that is the
ancestry of us all

It takes the Fierce Feminine to awaken in each
of us female and male
all her wisdom, love, mercy, and discernment
to be the catalyst for change in the world as
we know it

It takes the Fierce Feminine, whose Love fills the
heart of each of us
as we see every other through eyes of compassion
and understanding

It takes the Fierce Feminine to kneel at the Altar of
Gratitude with consciousness that the feminine
and the masculine deserve to live in
peace and harmony

It takes the Fierce Feminine to wrap her warrior
arms around us
in protection and love against the forces of
fear and rage

It takes the Fierce Feminine to demonstrate and
show kindness and mercy
to those who fight against love's reigning nature

It takes the Fierce Feminine to bow down in
reverence to the most
tenderhearted and vulnerable, for they will
inherit the earth and rule the world

It takes the Fierce Feminine to revel in the beauty
of the feminine and masculine
as they come together in the dance of union of
true goodness—
this will be the change we wish to see
in the world

It takes the Fierce Feminine to boldly hold
the opposite
as a purveyor of beauty and a sacred treasure
to behold

It takes the Fierce Feminine to challenge the status
quo and champion the immaturity of humanity
of the world to grow into their inherent wisdom

It takes the Fierce Feminine to be the
heart warrior
soul nurturer, slayer of lies, and the queen of truth

It takes the Fierce Feminine laying claim
to this revolutionary crack in the fabric of time,
breaking open the healing
ground-shaking-blinding-light-of-cosmic-
proportions promise of change

It takes the Fierce Feminine to birth this
Powerful

Generous
Kind
Beautiful
Lovely
Present
Tender
Passionate
Fearless
Ferocious
Nurturing
Empowering
Protective
Ancient
Embodied
Golden
Crown
Jewel
Life
Force
Into the world

It takes the Fierce Feminine
To surrender her heart for the good of the world
To take up arms to fight for our worth and value
To kneel down in prayer for what is good and
beautiful
To stand firm for the protection of the most
vulnerable

To gather arm-in-arm and to circle around,
providing love's embrace
To kneel at the feet of our opposite
To learn from them and hear their cries of pain
and suffering
To rise up and offer a gift of nourishment and
love
To heal the wound of their hurt
To at long last hold the hand and the heart of
someone you thought you knew only to know
them at their most vulnerable and sacred
To see the treasure within and bless it like it was
your own
being mirrored back to you in their struggling
eyes

That's what it takes
And the Fierce, Loving, Powerful, Compassionate
Feminine is the new way
Your heart will be held and valued as the
treasure it is
Whether you buy into the revolution or not
She loves you no matter and forever
Because at the heart of the Fierce Feminine is
Love Always Love!

Beauty Is

Beauty is the all-giving love of the Divine Mother
Beautiful too is the sweet strength she tends me in
the everyday of my life

Beauty is the carving into my soul the language of
love and forgiveness
Beautiful too is the mercy and grace afforded me
in the journey of love

Beauty is the grounded source depth of love
That tethers me to the truth of my truths
Beautiful too is the sacred source that vibrates in
the cells of my being
Awakening and coming alive again in this day

Beauty is the crying for deep sweet sound
soulfulness of my Mother's presence
Beautiful too is the cloak of light enveloping me
with her loving protection

Beauty is her soothing words—peace, ground,
blessed, beloved
Humbling me to my knees
Beautiful too is her invitation to stand in her
presence
As she knows no one who is her lesser but many
who are in service

Beauty is the sparkling of stars framing her face
As the halo of holiness illuminates the day
Beautiful too is the otherworldly illuminated awe
    that fills her presence
Radiating out, illuminating the darkness in the
    world

Beauty is the tiny spark of holiness touching me
And blessing me with her sovereignty
Beautiful too is the warmth of the Mother's love
    blessing me and my day

Alleluia!

Free your spirit so love can fill the air
Free your soul so love can fill your body
Free your essence so love can fill your heart
Free yourself so love can fill your world
Freedom rings in the truth of your being

You are the divine incarnate
You are the enchanting dervish
You are the sweet surrender
You are the soul seeing
You are the senses reeling

You are the mind chattering
You are the body wisdom
You are the heart rendering
You are the emotion expressing
You are the living awakening

You are the deadening dusk
You are the spirit singing
You are the fire igniting
You are the spark flying
You are the hope glimmering

You are the grounding matter ma
You are the holy blessing

You are the Universe in ecstatic motion
Alighting the stars of my constellation
Guiding me home to my humanity and my
holiness

You are the Amen to my Alleluia!

Sweet Delight

What do you have for me today, dear Death
   Mother?

Sweet delight as the stars
twinkle in the light of day

Sweet delight as the moon
reveals its rotund body to the morning dew

Sweet delight as the darkness
fades from my early morning sight

Sweet delight as the cape of slumber
awakens the body's senses

Sweet delight as the dreaming symbols
quiet in the rising sun

Sweet delight as the nothing of darkness
is illuminated by the divine light of my being

Sweet delight of the sleeping being
filled with the presence of the Divine Mother's
   Love.

Soul Speaks

Love Love Love
Sweet surrender
Death defying
Life reviving
Magical sparkle
Mystical trust
Majestic movement
Sound senses
Sustaining sweetness
Truthful expression
Vulnerable receiving
Lovely lessons
Truth embodied
Spiritual practice
Sacred grounding
Hallowed healing
Tender hearted
Delight deemed
Alleluia expressed
Amen declared
Essence landed
Soul Speaks

Joyous Delight

Joyous delight
Sweet surrender
Walk on the wild side
Heart rendering
Bountiful bravery
Courageous connection
Stunning presence
Hallowed eve
Awe inspiring
Veil lifting
Vulnerability held
Reverence abounding
Fierce feminine
Holy mother
Soul seekers
Soror Mystica sisters
Alleluia!

Sheer Pleasure

Sheer pleasure
Divine design
Soul yoga
Soft gaze
Sparkling essence
Grounded purity
Sweet connection
Powerful presence
Awe inspiring
Reverence rattling
Stunning beauty
Rockin' it
Soul shaking
Grace embodying
Courage abounding
Heart striking
Wowing wonder
Woo-hoo!

Arrival

Deep Love Deep Confusion

Rumi's "Love's confusing joy"
Swept into yourself
Stirred around your soul
Dusted up your sweetness

Washed away your doubt
Polished to a shine, your beauty
Cleansed like newly washed sheets flapping in
the wind
Your essence blaring its arrival to its newly
acquired home

Goddess Bless

Goddess bless
Blessed be
Blessed be
The light I see

Goddess bless
Blessed be
Blessed be
The love I see

Goddess bless
Blessed be
Blessed be
The spirit I see

Goddess bless
Blessed be
The water of life
The ground of soul
The air of breath
The light of love

Goddess bless
Blessed be

The love I feel in the heart of thee
The strength I feel in the body of thee
The instinctual wisdom I feel in the soul of thee
The truth I feel in the spirit of thee

Goddess bless
Blessed be
The essence I feel in the divine child in thee

Blessed be the toils and troubles through the
threshold to thee
Blessed be the miracles I see on the way to thee
Blessed be the gift of me as the mirror of thee
Blessed be the essence of me as the
daughter of thee
Blessed be the birthright of me as the
divine of thee

Goddess bless
Blessed be
Awomen

Notoriously Me

I want to be Notorious
Notorious for being me

The me that sings at the top of her lungs
and cannot hold a tune and does not care

The me that has the vocabulary of a well-
educated sailor
and the heart of a Sufi poet

The me that carries delight like a precious child
only sharing it with those whom she feels
loved by

The me that is a heart-rendering, soul-nurturing
adventurous wild woman rebel poet

The me that hears the Goddess calling for love
to be the remedy for what ails the world

The me that mirrors sacredness to the heartbroken
and loves them back to life

The me that strikes fear in the hearts of judgers
and naysayers
for they cannot deny bold vivid essence

The me that hears freedom ring and crosses
the threshold
into the unknown for love's sake

The me that dances like a dervish, getting lost
in the ecstatic prayer of our God-given bodies

The me that sings sweetly, praying to the Beloved
for light to enfold me and guide me home

The me that belly laughs unabashedly
with a take-no-prisoners kind of abandoned joy

The me that has a warrior spirit who can and does
fight the long fight for truth and beauty

The me that sheds a precious tear
every time sweetness caresses vulnerability and
soothes the beating heart

The me that drives me to do good in the world
and holds me now in softness and permission to
be me in all my brilliance

Blessed be the me that the Divine never let go of
guiding me every minute of every day to this
moment in time

Where freedom rings with me being me
The God-given child I was meant to be

Oh so notoriously me!

Miracle Among Miracles

You are a miracle among miracles
Take your place among the God-given!

Where sweetness surrenders and
Love abides the soul-whipping winds of change

Change the hearts bleeding
Into gold dust showering us with Love

Change the heartbreak
Into a million butterflies dancing along the breeze

Change the harrowing heaviness
Into the sweet smell of love's fragrance wafting
   through the air

Change the bolted door of your voice
Into the magical waterfall feeding a lush pool of
   water's refreshing truth

Change the crushing blows
Into the Earth-opening rush of mountains birthing
   new vistas

Change the severed senses
Into the wild winds of love, throwing open all the
   gateways to your soul

Change the lost and abandoned
Into the forever beauty of Mother Earth, letting
  her caress you back into being

You are a miracle among miracles
Take your place among the God-given!

Sweet Sacred Sovereignty

Sweet Sacred Sovereignty
Deeply flows within my skin
Like a clear life-giving water
Bathing me in sweetness

Sweet Sacred Sovereignty
Washes my heart
Cleansing me of the caked dirt
And purifying my senses

Sweet Sacred Sovereignty
Crashing waves upon the
Shores of my body
Brandishing me with
The strength of our Mothers

Sweet Sacred Sovereignty
Sweetly deeply embedded in my cells
Fashioning my soul

Sweet Sacred Sovereignty
Sacred ground source to the
Well of my being

Sweet Sacred Sovereignty
Sovereignty casting the circle

Where the rise of the Mothers
Of us all gather and cackle

Sweet Sacred Sovereignty
Sweet spells chanting in the dark
Rituals enacted for Sacred's sake

Sweet Sacred Sovereignty
Sacred dancing and spell casting
For sovereignty's Queen
To emerge in full regalia

Sweet Sacred Sovereignty
Sovereignty singing her heartfelt lament
For wisdom's reign to return
To the land of our souls

Sweet Sacred Sovereignty

Essence Prayer

May we hold our light as the Divine Mother holds
us in love and care
May we affirm our essence as the divine
birthright that it is
May we honor our divinity as the true origins
of our beauty
May we bless our hearts as we own the truth of
who we are
May we revel in our spirit one beautiful
blessing at a time
For we are here to be God and Goddesses'
children
Shining forth our beauty for the world
to be blessed

Soul Fury

You are the sparks that fly into the night sky
  reminding me of your divine fire

You are the gentle nod of understanding
  reminding me that you will always see truth
  and beauty

You are the twinkle in the eye of mirth and
  reverence
  reminding me that the Divine is chockful of
  pure delight

You are the laser-focused intention
  reminding me that you've got my back forever
  and always

You are the fury of the Soul creating anew every
  day
  reminding me of your fiery pure sweet essence

You are the true north on the compass
  reminding me that home is where the heart is

You are the deep abiding truth seer
  reminding me that beauty is in the eye of the
  beholder

You are the blessing of the Beloved
   anointing me with its magic every day of my life

May your soul fury continue to blaze trails to the
   heart
      and soul of what matters most

Happy day you were born, my starlit radiant sun
   magician

The Dangerous Truth

The dangerous truth
Sets you free from the confines of your inner
  prison
Challenges the status quo
Calls on the Gods for blessings

The dangerous truth
Sets the soul fury loose and
Acts on the soul's fiery wisdom
Rendering others senseless and running hither
  and thither

The dangerous truth
Wreaks havoc in the eyes of the beholder
Stuns the spiritual gawkers into silence and
Caresses the tiniest spark of essence into a
  roaring flame

The dangerous truth
Cajoles the unseen souls
Into active conduits of transformation
Shouting from the rooftops, "We are alive and
  well!"

The dangerous truth
Springs from the shadows

Dances alive the fiery truth
One twirl of salvation at a time

The dangerous truth
Rings through the airwaves, causing the winds to
    change direction
Breaks the hearts of the witnesses wide open,
    pouring forth tears of compassion
Shakes the unconscious and rocks all of the ages,
    for change is inevitable

The dangerous truth
Calls the fury to come alive in the act of speaking
    and
Softens even the hardest of hearts, pouring forth
    the dangerous truth
That women are alive and well and a force to be
    reckoned with
Full of dangerous, irreverent, trouble-making,
    soul-shaking, world-breaking truth

The dangerous truth
If you cannot hear it, perhaps you're not ready or
    able
But rest assured, you should do what you need to
    do to prepare yourself
A deep bow in reverence to the Feminine that
    birthed you would be a good start

The dangerous truth
Is an enlivening, enriching expression of your
 soul's essential wisdom
Let the soul's fiery truth burn away the old,
 encrusted, unjust untruths
And set you free, igniting your soul-reveling,
 spirit-shaking, earth-quaking Dangerous truth

Amen for the brave and daring truth tellers!

Anointed

Sweet remembering
Blessed beloved
Sweet remembrance warm love
Sunshine's golden rays

Joy's Child

Heart beating wildness
Ecstatic embracing love
Praise dancing dervish

Truth Charisma

True love astounding
Heartfelt beauty releasing
Pure delight yahoo

The Goddess Cafe

Love caught in the shadows of delight
Calling from the darkness, "I am here!"

Joy pushing its way to the front saying, "See me!"

Love stepping farther into the shadows
Resigning to the back of the crowd

Sweet sidles up next to Delight, blinking her eyes
In her coy way waiting to be seen

And Reverence standing fully in the front
Asking for silence and shooshing everybody

Awe lets out a big belly laugh
As she sits herself down for the festivities

Love once again tries to make her way to the front
Pushing and jostling around Holy and Wonder

Making her way to the front and center
Frustrated and shaking as she begins to sing her
enchanting song

With each note releasing the Divine's elixir and
magically everyone in attendance is enraptured

by the melody floating from Love's lips

Each and every one dancing and swaying
To her rhythmic resplendent melody

Ever grateful for her presence in their cabaret
Headlining at the Goddess Cafe!

Come on in, sit down, and enjoy the show
Maybe even you might take a turn at the mic
And be cheered and applauded for your
God-given gifts!

Wahoo and Cheers to you!

Sweet Talking

What do you have for me today, dear Death
  Mother?

I have a well of deep gratitude
My Sweet
I have a love beyond measure
My Moon Pie
I have an embracing delight
My Sweet Pea
I have a staggering swagger
My Darling
I have a panache-packed presence
My Angel Face
I have a bounty of treasures
My Sugar Pie
I have a sunrise full of sparkles
My Love Turtle
I have gorgeous banquet of love
My Miss Muffet
I have a kaleidoscope of kindness
My Peanut
I have a clambering of singing angels
My Lovie
I have a hearth of warming light
My Spitfire

How's that for what I have for you today, dear one?

Mothers' Daughters

Divinity Diving Deeply
Sweet Sorrow Surfacing
Ecstatic Elation Enveloping
Single Sound Swaying
Tender Teardrop Touching
Hearing Heaven's Harp
Passionate Prayer Playing
Bountiful Beauty Bewitching
Mirroring Mystical Magic
Goddess Gathering Ground
Women Wildly Weeping
Dancing Delight-Filled Divas
Power-Packing Purveyors
Truth Tangible Tellers
Eloquent Enigmatic Evermore

Sacred Mother

Holy Hallelujah
Hallowed healing spirit source
Heart of all hearts

Once Upon A Time

Once upon a time there was a girl who breathed
fire
Flew dragons and ate stars for snacks like candy

She carried a bow and arrow and shot untruth
clouds out of the sky
She wailed like a banshee, screaming love quotes
at the walking dead

She cracked a whip-garnering attention,
demanding a call to wake up
She tended the crescent moon and hung ribbons
Where blessings dangled from the ends for the
taking

She wielded a sword, striking wisdom into the
hearts of men
She showered in the rays of the sun, basking in
the illuminating warmth

She is now a fierce, grace-filled, gritty love
warrior, soul-nurturer
Card-carrying Mother's daughter feminine force
of nature
She births the sacred alive in this one now
moment

She coos and caresses and mirrors the beauty of
the Beloved to weary travelers
She is wild of heart and sings and dances like a
wicked dervish

She is a weaver of souls, a spinner of spells
Keeping the sacred flame alive in our hearts
She is the young, the old, the maiden, the mother,
the crone
The wise woman telling tales of triumphant
tragedies

She is the lightning strike in the darkness
Revealing flashes of intuition and insight
She is the lantern of light in the dark night
Keeping us from falling off the perilous path

Once upon a time she was a princess who knew
her strength and beauty
And walked it proudly into the light of day

And now, once upon this time, she is a queen
And in her domain she rules with soft caresses
And coaxes power and compassion through the
eye of the needle
To be sewn as threads of gold into the royal robes
of power

This once upon this time queen
Places the crown jewels of strength and beauty
Onto other once upon a time princesses
And straightens their crowns, reminding them in
  their heart of hearts
Whose daughters they really are

The Great Mother's, of course
Welcome home my once-upon-a-time princesses
How do your crowns fit?

Enchantment

I hear the spell of Mother Nature
Calling me home to Love
My Love has returned
My Love lives in my heart ...
Calling sweetness back into my body

My Love lives in my heart ...
Calling beauty back into my being
Calling energy up from my rooted soul
Calling love's embrace home from the depths of
  my being
Calling spirit's whirling blessing from my
  nourished senses
Calling me alive from the deadness of myself
Calling for truth and senses, soul and soothing,
  body and beloved
To come alive again in my being

Amen to rest and quiet and mountain vistas and
  nature's magical forests
And sacred sites and prayers written and left in
  the cracked walls of Mary's Grotto
And candles lit with petitions for peace in the
  Church of the natural
To walking and walking and walking on sacred
  ground

Surrounded by beauty and light of lights in the
    brightness of the day
Warming my body
Soothing my soul
And calling my Spirit alive in the quiet
    and solitude
In companionship with my Beloved
Healing me, I am Enchanted once again

Epilogue

Lessons Learned from Being Initiated by the Fierce Feminine

I am not defective because of what someone else says or does to me

I am more than my wounds—I have them but I am not them

I am a fighter and my super power is love, and I choose to use it for healing

I am fierce, strong, and capable

I have plumbed the depth of the cycle of transformation and lived to tell the tale

I can die and be reborn

I deserve love

I give and receive love

Love is for everyone, and not having it is the cause of most ills in life

Change is inevitable—I have learned to embrace it

I have learned to walk the path of transformation with grace and grit

I have learned if I am not betraying myself no one else can betray me

I have learned if I am listening to my instinctual wisdom and paying attention
to my deepest truth, life goes much smoother, cleaner, and clearer

I have learned to navigate in the moment and be a
   safe guide for those hurting
I have learned to use my strength for good in the
   world
I have learned to return to love, and I live
   practicing compassion whenever I am called to
I have learned to participate in the sacred
   contracts of my life experiences
I have learned to take only what I am responsible
   for, no more no less
I have learned when I am loved well I thrive
I have learned to commune with spirits and take
   delight in the Divine
I have learned many things from my betrayers,
   each having a mix of love and deep hurt
I have learned to release the bondage of pain and
   suffering
I have learned to mature into myself and not
   allow naiveté to hand my power over to others
I have learned that loving someone is a gift
It is not enough sometimes and it may be the very
   reason they betray us
   because they cannot bear that much love or
   meet us there in love
I have learned that they may need an exit strategy
And unfortunately, betrayal is an excellent exit
   strategy

I have learned that love should not be given
  haphazardly or naively
It needs to be given to another with respect and
  honor as the precious gift and treasure it is
I have learned to replace the hurt and wounds
  with Love and Peace and Power and Grace
I have learned that this earthly existence is
  perfectly imperfect
  if I can garner the wisdom from the Universe's
  lessons
I have learned there is mystery and magic
  if I can open my heart and my eyes to see
I have learned that gratitude is a mind bender and
  a soul renderer to a peaceful way of living
I have learned that fear is a very bad guide and
  shame an even worse navigator
I have learned that our essence is just underneath
  the surface
  of our coping strategies, ready to be recovered
  like a diamond from a cave
I have learned that it takes some serious mining
  to get at it
I have learned that forgiveness affords me a
  freedom that knows no bounds
I have learned that delight blows up any and all
  devastation
I have learned that laughter and sorrow cannot
  exist in the same moment

I have learned that my wounds have been the
greatest gift for my growth as a woman
I have learned that I am who the Goddess and
God intended me to be
I have learned that a revolution of love begins
within me

I pray that your journey yields your highest
learnings for your highest good
and that you find the Fierce Feminine within
you and allow her to lovingly guide you every
step of the way to your brilliant notorious self

Happy Trails to you!
Lizanne

Here's What I Know Today,
Dear Death Mother

(For my dear friends Neil and Vanessa and for all of us who are facing death and supporting the last vestiges of a life well lived.)

What I know is that life can be as high as a kite,
enjoying its freedom flight in the beautiful of the
blue sky

What I know is that in an instant of the news that
cancer is a friend's
unwanted companion, that news can and does
strip all joy out of every cell
of my being and drop me into deep dark sorrow

What I know is that tending to the everyday is a
matter of course
and hope is the tiny ray of light that helps me
manage through the dark matter

What I know is that the deep ache in my soul is
grief being held at bay
with the gatekeeper allowing tiny snippets
through at a time, so the
onslaught of grief doesn't drown me in sorrow's
tears

What I know is that the hollowed-out hole I feel
   in the core of my being
   just by anticipating the loss to our world with
   my friend's presence leaving
   feels like an anchor dropping me to the bottom
   of the ocean
   in echoing silence with no air to breathe

What I know is that I know this too well and I
   don't want to know death
   as a familiar companion right now; I do not
   want him sitting silently
   beside me, haunting my day with the reality
   of losing my friend

What I know is that while deep sorrow brings me
   to my knees, deep strength
   and faith raise me up to hold what needs to be
   held for my beloved ones
   who are suffering

What I know is that my heart is broken, shattered
   into tiny pieces, like a mirror
   that has been smashed, and I am desperately
   trying to glue the slivers and
   shards back together, so I can see my friend
   again as whole and here

What I know is that I want the clock to rewind to
the before of the moment
of when the news of cancer catapulted me
forward into the reality of
losing my friend

What I know is that I want a moment of peace,
when all is right with the
world and we'll deal with whatever comes our
way, before the future
is ripped so ferociously from my heart

What I want is to not see the film in my head of
the days, weeks, and months
ahead of us, where loss is our constant heralder
of bad news

What I want is love, pure love, as much as can
possibly be mustered
to fill the hole in my gut so my friends know
that love outshines,
outlasts, out-maneuvers, and is eternal and
forever between us

What I want is for love to surround my friends
and carry them in grace
and faith on this next stretch of their journey

What I want them to know is that I will be
   available at every weigh station
   and stop to offer love in whatever way they may
   need it—whether they need
   floors scrubbed, clothes washed, errands run, or
   someone to sit with
   them—whatever they need, I've got them!

What I want is for them to know they don't ever
   have to walk this path alone—
   we can and will, so choose to be present as
   much as they need or want us to be

What I want is for love to surround them, bless
   them, comfort and hold them
That's what I know and what I want dear
   Death Mother.

In deep abiding love,
Lizanne

Final Note from the Author

I thank all of you heart warriors for your courage, fortitude, righteous and soul-reveling work of healing and laying claim to your notorious selves. For it takes the Fierce Feminine in all her big, bold love to transform the world.

So, look out world, here we come! All the heart warriors of the Fierce Feminine spreading our unique brand of brilliance as beacons of light for all to see and be blessed by! Being notoriously ourselves and healing each other and the world through love—always love.

Special Acknowledgments

To my beloved husband, Craig Tessem, who inspires and encourages me with his wit and wisdom. Always championing me to be the sacred rebel poet. Thank you my beloved.

To my book crew who, through trials and challenges, kept things moving and aligned to true north, even when the road was rocky:

Andrea Costantine, the consummate navigator and designer of dreams.

Donna Mazzitelli, the exquisite editor and heart warrior of words.

Delta Donohue, the generous grace-bestowing guide.

Each of you has blessed me and this book with your fiercely beautiful presence and expertise. Thank you. I am blessed to have you as part of my tribe of fiercely feminine women.

To the reader, may you embrace your fierce love and show the world how it's done.

About the Author

Lizanne Corbit M.A., L.P.C. is a psychotherapist in private practice in Denver, where she lives and enjoys life with her husband, Craig. Lizanne is a heart warrior, soul nurturer, rebel poet, and a midwife to the spirit. She guides others to their inner brilliance in her private practice, women's groups, and as a co-facilitator of the transformational process of Soul Speaks, helping people change the world by being themselves.

Lizanne is here to help you learn how to navigate the life crises that come from the inevitable changes we all experience throughout our lives. Some change we see coming and welcome; some change rattles us, because we never expect or see it coming; but all crises call us to be more of who we are. Lizanne helps you not only hear but answer the call to be more of who you are.

Lizanne guides you on your "peregrine," your sacred journey, where you'll mine for the gold that is your inner beauty to uncover and reclaim the "Instatus Nascendi," the jewels hidden in matter—your inner brilliance. Lizanne guides you to love yourself so fiercely that you can't help but bring your unique one-of-a-kind, special-beyond-measure brand of inner brilliance into the world.

Lizanne loves to perform her poetry, sharing the message of the Divine Feminine from her books, *Night Star: Reflections on the Path of The Divine Feminine* and *Notorious: Poetic Travels of the Fierce Feminine.*

Contact with Lizanne:
LizanneCorbitCounselingDenver.com
LizanneCorbit@gmail.com

Made in the
USA
Middletown, DE